CAMBRIDGE

AMERICAN EMPOWER

WORKBOOK WITH ANSWERS

T0306673

A2

ELEMENTARY

Peter Anderson

CONTENTS

Contents

1A I'M FROM FRANCE

1 GRAMMAR *be*: affirmative and negative

a Underline the correct forms of the verb *be*.

1 I *'s* / *'re* / *<u>'m</u>* Brazilian.
2 They *'re* / *'m* / *'s* from Barcelona.
3 He *'e* / *'s* / *'m* with his Spanish friends.
4 We *'s* / *'m* / *'re* American.
5 Rome *'m* / *'re* / *'s* a beautiful city.
6 It *'re* / *'s* / *'m* very hot in August.

b Complete each sentence with a negative form of the verb *be*. Use contractions. (Sometimes there is more than one possible answer.)

1 The Italian team _'s not / isn't_ very good at the moment.
2 My brother ________ at the party. He's here.
3 My sister and I ________ Brazilian. We're Mexican.
4 I ________ Spanish. I'm Italian.
5 They ________ from Rome. They're from Milan.
6 Tomomi ________ Chinese. She's Japanese.
7 You ________ from Hamburg. You're from Berlin.
8 Mike ________ at a party. He's at a concert.

2 VOCABULARY Countries and nationalities

a Complete the sentences with the correct nationalities.

1 He's _Ecuadorian_.

2 She's ________.

3 He's ________.

4 They're ________.

5 She's ________.

6 She's ________.

7 She's ________.

8 They're ________.

b Complete the crossword puzzle.

→ Across

4 Argentina, Brazil, and Venezuela are all in _South America_.
7 ________ is the home of flamenco dancing and paella.
10 Mount Fuji is in ________.
11 Paris, Lyon, and Marseilles are all in ________.

↓ Down

1 Rio de Janeiro is in ________.
2 Moscow is the capital city of ________.
3 Wolfgang, Hans, and Petra are from Berlin in ________.
5 Sydney and Melbourne are cities in ________.
6 Florence, Rome, and Venice are all in ________.
8 The capital of ________ is Beijing.
9 The capital of ________ isn't Istanbul. It's Ankara.

3 PRONUNCIATION Syllables and word stress

a 01.01 Listen and complete the chart with the words in the box. Then underline the stressed syllable in each word.

~~Turkish~~ Irish Japanese Saudi American Russian Mexican Nigerian Colombian

2 syllables	3 syllables	4 syllables
<u>Tur</u>kish		

1B SHE'S A WONDERFUL PERSON

1 GRAMMAR
be: questions and short answers

a Underline the correct words to complete the questions.

1 Where *you are* / *are you* / *is you* from?
2 *Is he* / *He is* / *Are he* married?
3 *Are she* / *She is* / *Is she* from Mexico?
4 *You are* / *You is* / *Are you* here with your family?
5 *Is you* / *Are you* / *You are* Turkish?
6 What *their names are* / *is their names* / *are their names*?
7 *Are Enzo* / *Is Enzo* / *Enzo is* Spanish?
8 *Is Joe and Mel* / *Joe and Mel are* / *Are Joe and Mel* American?

b Complete each short answer with the correct form of *be*. Use contractions where possible. (Sometimes there is more than one possible answer.)

1 **A** Are you Brazilian?
B Yes, I am.
2 **A** Is David a good tennis player?
B No, ________.
3 **A** Are you and your brother here on vacation?
B No, ________.
4 **A** Is New York a friendly city?
B Yes, ________.
5 **A** Are you from Mexico City?
B No, ________.
6 **A** Is Julia American?
B Yes, ________.
7 **A** Are your friends cool?
B Yes, ________.
8 **A** Are Alan and Sue here today?
B No, ________.

2 VOCABULARY Adjectives

a 01.02 Listen and complete the sentences with the words in the box.

great fantastic cool amazing wonderful ~~warm~~
friendly pleasant kind well known quiet popular

1 I like Jane. She's a warm and ________ person.
2 Our new teacher's really ________ and he's very ________ with his students.
3 Marisa's a ________ singer. She's really ________ in Portugal.
4 My friend Sarah's a ________ person. She's really ________ to all her friends.
5 Alicia is very ________, but she's a ________ friend.
6 Mr. Jones is a very ________ person, and he's an ________ teacher.

b Complete the sentences with the words in 2a.

1 New York is a fantastic city. I love it!
2 My father's an a________g doctor.
3 He's a very w____l-k____n singer in my country. He's really p______r with young people.
4 I think your brother's really c____l. He's a g____t guitarist.
5 My friend Anna's very f________y. She's a really w________l person.
6 John's a very q______t person. He's always k____d to animals.

3 PRONUNCIATION
Sound and spelling: /k/

a Do the words in the chart have a /k/ sound? Check (✓) the correct column.

	/k/ sound	No /k/ sound
chat		✓
cake		
keep		
know		
quiz		
capital		
bike		
chart		

b 01.03 Listen and check.

1C EVERYDAY ENGLISH
What's your last name?

1 USEFUL LANGUAGE
Asking for and giving information

a Put the words in the correct order to make sentences.

1 help / I / can / how / you ?
How can I help you?
2 to take / like / I'd / a fitness class .
______
3 last name / your / what's ?
______
4 you / please / spell / that, / can ?
______
5 class / the / time's / next / what ?
______
6 at / tomorrow / it's / six thirty .
______
7 class / the / where's ?
______
8 Room / 3 / in / it's .
______
9 6:30 / in / that's / Room / 3 / so ?
______
10 help / for / thanks / your .
______
11 welcome / you're .
______

b 01.04 Listen and check.

c Put the conversation in the correct order.

☐ No problem. We have great German classes for beginners.
☐ Gonzales.
☐ When are the classes?
1 Hello. How can I help you?
☐ They're on Mondays at 7:30.
☐ Sure. What's your last name?
☐ Can you spell that, please?
☐ Hi. I'd like to take a German class. I'm a beginner.
☐ Great. I'm free on Monday evenings. Can I sign up for the class?
☐ Thank you. Enjoy the class.
☐ G-O-N-Z-A-L-E-S.

d 01.05 Listen and check.

2 PRONUNCIATION
Intonation for checking; Consonant clusters

a 01.06 Listen to each speaker. Does the intonation go up (↗) or down (↘)? Check (✓) the correct box.

	↗	↘
1 Absolutely.	☐	✓
2 Good idea.	☐	☐
3 Me?	☐	☐
4 Sure.	☐	☐
5 Off to the gym?	☐	☐
6 Of course.	☐	☐
7 Is he from London?	☐	☐
8 Yes, he is.	☐	☐
9 Is she Argentinian?	☐	☐
10 No, she's not.	☐	☐
11 No problem.	☐	☐

b 01.07 Listen and write the number of consonant sounds in each word.

1 [2] three
2 ☐ eight
3 ☐ twelve
4 ☐ sixteen
5 ☐ right
6 ☐ match
7 ☐ brother
8 ☐ warm
9 ☐ kitchen
10 ☐ well known

1D SKILLS FOR WRITING
I'm Carla and I'm from Mexico

1 READING

a Dmitri is taking an English class in New York City. Read his fact file on the language school website and check (✓) the correct answers.

1 Which country is Dmitri from?
- a ☐ Poland
- b ☐ Turkey
- c ☐ Greece
- d ☐ Russia

2 Which city is Dmitri from?
- a ☐ New York City
- b ☐ Moscow
- c ☐ St. Petersburg
- d ☐ Lomonosov

FACT FILE

Name: Dmitri Bolshov
Age: 20
Nationality: Russian
Lives in: Moscow
Hometown: St. Petersburg
Job/Occupation: Student, Lomonosov Moscow State University
Likes: languages, music, running

b Read Dmitri's personal profile. Are the sentences true or false?

1 Dmitri's 20 years old.
2 Dmitri studies in St. Petersburg.
3 Dmitri's in the U.K. with friends from Moscow.
4 Dmitri's taking a computer class in New York City.
5 Dmitri likes listening to music.

Personal profile

This is Dmitri Bolshov. He's 20 years old and he's Russian. He's from St. Petersburg, but he studies at Lomonosov Moscow State University. It's his first time in the U.S., and he's taking an English class in New York City with a big group of friends from Moscow. He's very happy to be in New York City. He likes languages, music, and running.

2 WRITING SKILLS
Capital letters and punctuation

a Correct the personal profile about Carlos. Add capital letters and punctuation (., ').

Personal profile

This is carlos ferreira hes 35 years old and hes brazilian hes from petrópolis but he studies languages he takes spanish classes in bogotá this isnt his first time in colombia hes very happy to be in bogotá he likes languages movies and jazz

This is ______________________
____
____

3 WRITING

a Complete the fact file with information about a friend, a family member, or a famous person.

FACT FILE

Name: ______________
Age: ______________
Nationality: ______________
Lives in: ______________
Hometown: ______________
Job/Occupation: ______________
Likes: ______________

b Use the information in the fact file to write a personal profile about this person. Remember to use capital letters and punctuation in the correct places.

This is ______________________
____
He/She likes ______________________
____

UNIT 1
Reading and listening extension

1 READING

a Read the letter. What are these parts of the letter about? Check (✓) the correct answers.

Paragraph 1 is about …
a ☐ Elena's dogs.
b ☑ Elena and her mom.
c ☐ Elena's sister.
d ☐ Elena's dad.

Paragraph 2 is about …
a ☐ Elena's dogs.
b ☐ Elena and her mom.
c ☐ Elena's sister.
d ☐ Elena's dad.

Paragraph 3 is about …
a ☐ Elena's dogs.
b ☐ Elena and her mom.
c ☐ Elena's sister.
d ☐ Elena's dad.

Paragraph 4 is about …
a ☐ Elena's dogs.
b ☐ Elena and her mom.
c ☐ Elena's sister.
d ☐ Elena's dad.

b Read the letter again. Are the sentences true or false?

1 The letter is to Elena's Mexican friend.
2 The family of Elena's mom lives in Mexico.
3 Elena's dad is awful.
4 Elena and her family go to Mexico every year.
5 Elena's mom's family has a lot of money.
6 Elena's sister isn't very good at tennis.
7 Elena loves her dogs.
8 Elena wants Ofelia to write to her again.

c Write a letter to a new friend in Japan.

- Write about each person in your family.
- How many people live in your house? Who are they?
- Where does your family go on vacation?

Dear ______________________________

____

____

____

____

____

____

____

____

____

____

Dear Ofelia,

Thanks for your letter. It's really interesting for me to hear about your life in Ecuador.

1 Here is a photo of my family. It's a pretty new photo, so you can see what we all look like. As you can see, I have dark hair, and so does my mom. She's from Mexico.

2 My dad's pretty quiet, but he's very kind, and he often helps me with my homework. He's American – that's why we live here in Florida. Every summer we visit my mom's family in Mexico. Her parents aren't rich, but they have a beautiful house near the beach. I love it!

3 You can see my sister next to me. She has a lot of friends, and she's very popular. She's also a great tennis player. In fact, she's not at home very often because she plays tennis so much!

4 At the front of the photo, you can see two other important members of our family. They're very old, and they're not very clean, but I love them. They're my dogs, Benny and Jerry!

Write back soon and tell me more about your family!

Talk soon,

Elena

2 LISTENING

a 01.08 Listen to the conversation. Check (✓) the best endings for the sentences.

1 Charlie and Pedro …
  a ☐ know each other well.
  b ☑ don't know each other well.

2 They play on …
  a ☐ the same soccer team.
  b ☐ the same basketball team.

3 Charlie says that Pedro …
  a ☐ can go to the next soccer game with him.
  b ☐ can take him to the next soccer game.

b 01.08 Listen to the conversation again. Complete the sentences with the words in the box.

doesn't have	plays	ready	speaks
game	~~soccer~~	grandma	Mexican

1 Pedro and Charlie meet on a ___*soccer*___ team.
2 Pedro is from Mazatlán. He's ___________.
3 Charlie's ___________ is also Mexican.
4 Charlie ___________ Spanish, but not very well.
5 Charlie ___________ soccer with the team every week.
6 The ___________ next week is in Albany.
7 Pedro ___________ a car.
8 Pedro must be ___________ by 9 o'clock.

c Write a conversation between two people who meet each other. Remember to say:

- where they are from
- what they like doing in their free time.

Review and extension

1 GRAMMAR

Underline and correct the mistake in each sentence.

1 My mother and father <u>is</u> from Maine. *are*
2 She really's friendly.
3 Daniela are Ecuadorian.
4 Im' from Bogotá, the capital of Colombia.
5 You are American or Canadian?
6 There from San Francisco.
7 **A** Is you and your friends Mexican?
  B No, we not.
8 **A** Are Maria from Rio de Janeiro?
  B Yes, she's.

2 VOCABULARY

Correct the mistake in each sentence.

1 My vacation in Jamaica was wonderfull. *wonderful*
2 New York is an amaizing city!
3 My best friend Nick's a really kool guy.
4 The weather is terible, but our vacation is great!
5 This is Anna. She's very frendly.
6 My mom likes Michael. She thinks he's very neice!
7 Nashville's a fantastik place to visit.
8 His uncle is pour, but he's very happy.

3 WORDPOWER *from*

Match 1–6 with a–f to make sentences.

1 My sister and I are
2 Dinner is
3 The train station is about 2 km
4 Are you
5 The next yoga class is
6 The train

a from Seattle is now at Platform 25.
b from 10:30 to 12:00 in the studio.
c from Washington or New York?
d from the Red Roof Inn.
e from Australia.
f from 7:00 to 10:00 at the Sorrento Restaurant.

REVIEW YOUR PROGRESS

Look again at Review Your Progress on p. 18 of the Student's Book. How well can you do these things now?
3 = very well   2 = well   1 = not so well

I CAN …	
talk about where I'm from	☐
talk about people I know	☐
ask for and give information	☐
write an online profile.	☐

2A SHE LOVES HER JOB

1 GRAMMAR Simple present: affirmative and negative

a <u>Underline</u> the correct words to complete the sentences.

1 I'm a nurse in a hospital, so I often *works* / <u>*work*</u> / *working* at night.
2 We're always really busy, so we *don't have* / *doesn't have* / *not have* time to go to the supermarket during the week.
3 Jake studies hard in the morning, so he *relax* / *relaxing* / *relaxes* for half an hour after lunch.
4 Sonia *not have* / *don't have* / *doesn't have* a very interesting job.
5 Joe's not very interested in sports, so he *doesn't watch* / *don't watch* / *watch not* soccer games on TV.
6 We work hard during the week, so we usually *relaxes* / *relax* / *relaxing* on the weekends.

b Complete the sentences with the correct forms of the verbs in parentheses. Use contractions where possible.

1 My father doesn't drive (not drive) to work. He always goes (go) by bus.
2 She ________ (not like) her job because she ________ (not make) much money.
3 I ________ (not like) my college math class because I ________ (think) it's really boring.
4 My drive to work only ________ (take) about 20 minutes, and I usually ________ (start) work at 8:30.

2 VOCABULARY Jobs

a Complete the crossword puzzle.

→ Across

2 Carol works as a tour guide at the Statue of Liberty.
4 My sister's a ________ ________, so some people think her job is very dangerous.
6 A typical New York City ________ ________ drives for eight hours a day.
7 A ________ works in a hospital.
8 My dad is a ________ for American Airlines.
9 David's a well-known ________. He lives in Hollywood now.

↓ Down

2 The ________ at this hotel is really friendly and helpful.
3 He's a famous ________ and he works in a really expensive restaurant in Paris.
4 Magazines use a ________ to take photos of famous people.
5 My brother works at the Volkswagen repair shop as a ________.

3 PRONUNCIATION Word stress

a 02.01 Which syllable is stressed in the words in **bold**? Listen and check (✓) the correct stress.

1 She works as a **receptionist** in a big hotel.
a ☑ re<u>cep</u>tionist b ☐ reception<u>ist</u>
2 He's a Colombian **businessman**.
a ☐ business<u>man</u> b ☐ <u>bus</u>inessman
3 My father's an **engineer**.
a ☐ engi<u>neer</u> b ☐ <u>en</u>gineer
4 Jack works as a **mechanic** for Toyota.
a ☐ me<u>chan</u>ic b ☐ <u>me</u>chanic
5 My uncle's a **taxi driver** in Mexico City.
a ☐ taxi dri<u>ver</u> b ☐ <u>ta</u>xi driver
6 Brad Pitt's a well known American **actor**.
a ☐ <u>ac</u>tor b ☐ ac<u>tor</u>
7 My **secretary** speaks excellent English.
a ☐ secre<u>tar</u>y b ☐ <u>sec</u>retary
8 She works as a **tour guide** in Los Angeles.
a ☐ tour <u>guide</u> b ☐ <u>tour</u> guide
9 He's a very friendly **police officer**.
a ☐ po<u>lice</u> officer b ☐ police <u>of</u>ficer
10 Where's the **photographer**?
a ☐ <u>pho</u>tographer b ☐ pho<u>tog</u>rapher

4 PRONUNCIATION -*s* endings

a 02.02 Listen and complete the chart with the verbs in the box.

~~watches~~ likes goes stops uses finishes plays teaches works freezes

The verb has an extra syllable: /ɪz/	The verb doesn't have an extra syllable: /s/ or /z/
watches	

2B DO YOU WORRY ABOUT EXAMS?

1 GRAMMAR Simple present: questions and short answers

a Underline the correct words to complete the sentences.

1 **A** *You like* / <u>*Do you like*</u> / *Like you* your new job?
  B Yes, *I does* / *I like* / *I do*.
2 **A** *Study Angela* / *Angela studies* / *Does Angela study* on Sundays?
  B No, *she no studies* / *she doesn't* / *she don't*.
3 What *do they do* / *do they* / *they do* in their free time?
4 How many hours a week *study you* / *you study* / *do you study* English?
5 **A** *Does he have* / *He has* / *Has he* important exams at school this year?
  B Yes, *he has* / *he does* / *he is*.
6 **A** *Listen you* / *Do you listen* / *You listen* to podcasts while you study?
  B No, *I not listen* / *I listen not* / *I don't*.

b Put the words in the correct order to make questions.

1 you / in your free time / do / what / do ?
  What do you do in your free time?
2 you / study / do / for your exams / late at night ?
  ____
3 you / music / do / while you study / to / listen ?
  ____
4 at the end / exams / have / do / of this year / they / important ?
  ____
5 have / how many days a week / she / does / class ?
  ____

2 VOCABULARY Studying

a Complete the sentences with the words in the box.

schedule break notes grade study exams ~~semester~~

1 At our school the summer semester is 12 weeks long.
2 I hate taking ______ because I'm not very good at them.
3 Joe has a new ______ for his English class. He has classes on Mondays, Wednesdays, and Fridays from 11:30 to 1:00.
4 Sarah always gets a good ______ on her math tests. She's so good at math!
5 It's important to take ______ in your notebook when you are in your English classes.
6 The computer class is from 9:30 to 12:30, but we usually have a ______ at 11 o'clock.
7 Do you ______ with your classmates?

3 VOCABULARY Time

a Match the clocks with the times in the box.

a quarter to nine nine thirty five to nine
twenty-five after nine a quarter after nine
~~five after nine~~ nine o'clock twenty-five to nine

1 five after nine

2 ______

3 ______

4 ______

5 ______

6 ______

7 ______

8 ______

2C EVERYDAY ENGLISH
I'd like a latte

1 USEFUL LANGUAGE
Asking for things and replying

a Match sentences 1–6 with responses a–f.

1 [c] Could I come to your place tonight?
2 [ ] Can I call you tomorrow?
3 [ ] I'd like some help with my car.
4 [ ] Can I have a hot chocolate, please?
5 [ ] Could we meet at 4:15?

a Of course. Small or large?
b Sure. Is it in the parking lot?
c Sorry, we're not at home.
d Sorry, I have a meeting at 4 o'clock.
e Sure, no problem. Call me around 10 o'clock.

b Complete the short conversations with the words in the box.

sorry could you I'd like I'm really ~~can I have~~ doesn't matter of course too bad no problem could we

1 **A** Can I have a small coffee, please?
B ________. Would you like cream or sugar?
2 **A** ________ some help with my homework, please.
B ________, not now. I'm busy.
A That's OK. It ________.
3 **A** ________ pass me my phone, please?
B Sure, ________. Here you go.
4 **A** ________ meet tomorrow morning?
B ________ sorry. I'm not available then.
A Oh, well, that's ________.

c 02.03 Listen and check.

2 PRONUNCIATION
Sound and spelling: *ou*

a 02.04 Listen to the words with *ou* and complete the chart with the words in the box.

~~pound~~ count pour mouse four loud

/ɔ/ (e.g., c**our**se)	/aʊ/ (e.g., h**ou**se)
	pound

2D SKILLS FOR WRITING
I need English for my job

1 READING

a Read Juliana's competition entry form and check (✓) the reason she needs English in her job.

1 ☐ Because she now works in Rio Grande.
2 ☐ Because she has a new job in the hotel.
3 ☐ Because the hotel guests don't all speak Portuguese.
4 ☐ Because her manager doesn't speak English.

b Read the competition entry form again. Are the sentences true or false?

1 Juliana doesn't like working as a hotel receptionist.
2 The guests want to speak Portuguese to her.
3 Sometimes it's hard for her to understand the guests.
4 She doesn't need to use the phone very much.
5 She would like to learn more words so she can help tourists.

Competition entry form

First name: Juliana Last name: Gomes
Gender: ✓ female ☐ male Nationality: Brazilian
Your class now: 8C Class start date: 05/04/24

Why is English important for you?

I work as a hotel receptionist in Rio de Janeiro. I like my job. I'm always busy, and the guests are nice and friendly. But most of them don't speak very good Portuguese. They all want to speak in English, and my English isn't very good.

What's difficult for you?

The guests speak quickly, and I don't understand them. It's difficult to answer. So learning English is very important for my job.

What do you want to improve in your English?

I use the phone a lot at work, so I need to improve my listening and speaking. I also want to improve my grammar and learn more vocabulary to help tourists in my city. I'd like to stay in the U.S. for another month to improve my English.

2 WRITING SKILLS Spelling

a Correct the spelling of the words in **bold**.

1 What's your home **adress**, please? _address_
2 Samantha **nose** a lot about computers. ______
3 We always have a **brake** for 15 minutes in the middle of our English class. ______
4 I think it's very **dificult** to study Spanish and Portuguese at the same time. ______
5 What time do you want to **meat** me after work? ______
6 I would like to see the new James Bond movie next **weak**. ______
7 My **farther** works as a doctor in Bogotá. ______

3 WRITING

a Antonio Morales is a business student from Ecuador. He studies English and Business in Los Angeles. There is a competition to win ten free language classes. Use the information below to complete the entry form for him.

Personal information

Email: morales_a@cup.org
Class: 8B
Class start date: 09/01/24
Hometown: Quito, Ecuador
Job: Business student
Why he needs English: make friends, read books, pass a business exam in English
Problems: some difficult words, people speak fast
Wants to improve: listening, speaking, writing essays (spelling is difficult!)

LOS ANGELES UNIVERSITY
LANGUAGE CENTER COMPETITION ENTRY FORM

First name: ______ Last name: ______
Gender: ◯ female ◯ male Nationality: ______
Email: ______ Class: ______

Why is English important for you?

English is important for me because ______
______
______

What's difficult for you?

______
______
______

What do you want to improve in your English?

______
______
______

UNIT 2
Reading and listening extension

1 READING

a Read the text and underline the correct words to complete the sentences.

1 Irene *likes* / *doesn't like* her job.
2 She *wants* / *doesn't want* to be a janitor for her whole life.
3 She *works* / *doesn't work* the whole day.

b Complete the sentences about the text. Use the words in the box.

at the end of the day ~~early in the morning~~
in the afternoon in the middle of the day

1 Irene starts work early in the morning.
2 She finishes work ______.
3 She goes to school ______.
4 She studies ______.

c Read the text again. Are the sentences true or false?

1 Irene thinks that most people want to be janitors.
2 There are a lot of people and cars in the streets at 6 o'clock in the morning.
3 Irene likes to hear the birds.
4 She doesn't do very much at work.
5 She talks to the nurses in the hospital.
6 She wants to be a doctor.
7 She takes night classes.
8 She doesn't have time for her studies.

d Write a paragraph about one job you want to do and one job you don't want to do. Think about these questions:

- What are the good things about the job you want to do? Why do you like those things?
- What are the bad things about the job you don't want to do? Why don't you like those things?

Irene's story

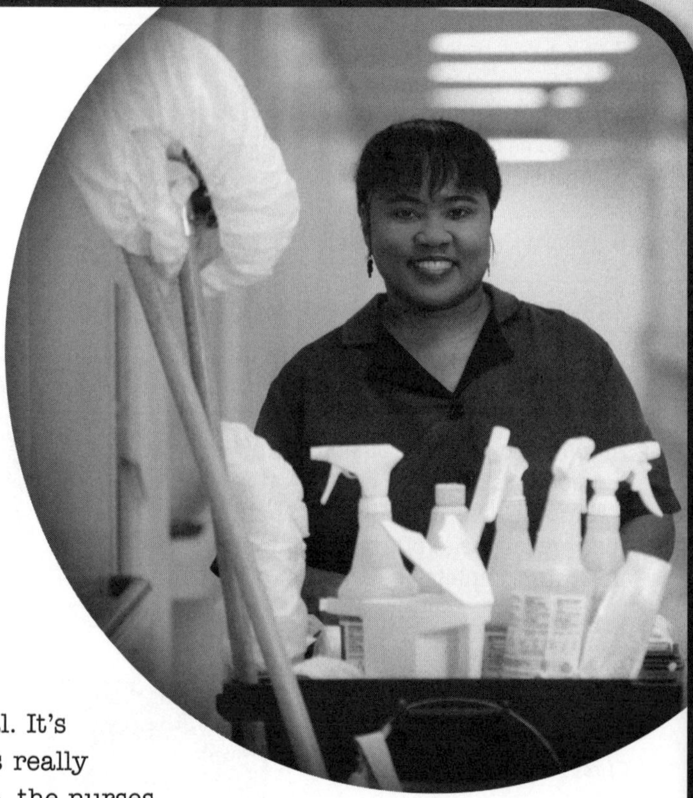

I'm a janitor. I love my job. I'm sure you're surprised to hear that. You probably don't know anyone who wants to become a janitor!

So why do I love my job? Well, first, I start work at 6 o'clock. When I walk to work, the streets are quiet, and I can hear the birds sing. You don't usually hear the birds in the middle of the city!

The second thing is, I work in a hospital. It's hard work, but I know that what I do is really helpful, and that makes me happy. Also, the nurses are friendly, and I chat with them when I have time.

But I don't want to be a janitor my whole life. I really want to be an engineer. I take classes in the evenings.

That's why the third reason is the really important one. I finish work at lunch time! So when everyone else goes back to work after their lunch break, I have time to study.

2 LISTENING

a ▶02.05 Listen to the conversation. Check (✓) the things Alex and Dan talk about.

- [✓] school
- [ ] exams
- [ ] sports
- [ ] food
- [ ] jobs
- [ ] their dads

b Complete the sentences about the conversation. Use *wants* or *doesn't want*.

1 Alex doesn't want to work in his dad's store.
2 Alex ____________ more time to study.
3 Dan ____________ to study less.
4 Dan ____________ to be a pilot.
5 Dan ____________ to be a photographer.
6 Dan ____________ to take photos of famous people.
7 Dan's dad ____________ to pay for him to become a photographer.
8 Dan ____________ Alex to say the same things as his dad.

c Write a conversation between two people talking about their studies and what jobs they want to do. Think about these questions:

- Do they work hard?
- Do they enjoy their studies?
- What job do they want?
- Do their parents agree?

Review and extension

1 GRAMMAR

Correct the sentences.

1 They starts work at 9:00 on Saturdays.
They start work at 9:00 on Saturdays.
2 Julia study hard on weekends.
3 She speak Portuguese and Spanish very well.
4 Sam and Ian doesn't likes exams.
5 Do she finish work late?
6 Does Jacob and Sara have a math class at 2:30?
7 My father work as a taxi driver.
8 We knows a lot about computers.

2 VOCABULARY

Correct the sentences.

1 My maneger is great. She's a very kind person.
My manager is great. She's a very kind person.
2 Mrs. Carr works as a recepsionist at the hospital.
3 He's an American businesman.
4 My cousin's a police in Louisiana.
5 Graciela Iturbide's a famous Mexican fotograf.
6 Max works at a five-star hotel as a sheff.
7 The drivers taxi in Lima always go very fast.
8 My friend's a mekanik and he fixes my old car for free.

3 WORDPOWER *work*

Underline the correct words to complete the sentences.

1 I start / go work at 8:30 in the morning.
2 My father works *for* / *as* a sales manager *for* / *in* Speedy Computer Solutions.
3 Sylvia works *for* / *as* a nurse *as* / *in* a big hospital in Chicago.
4 I need to find a new job because I'm *at* / *out of* work at the moment.
5 Sorry, I can't text you when I'm *at* / *in* work.
6 Sometimes I *go to* / *go* work by car, but I usually walk.

REVIEW YOUR PROGRESS

Look again at Review Your Progress on p. 28 of the Student's Book. How well can you do these things now?
3 = very well 2 = well 1 = not so well

I CAN ...	
talk about jobs	☐
talk about study habits	☐
ask for things and reply	☐
complete a form.	☐

3A SHE OFTEN TAKES AN ENGLISH CLASS

1 GRAMMAR Position of adverbs of frequency

a Underline the correct words to complete the sentences.

1 I *catch usually* / *usually catch* the bus to school, and I *am always* / *always am* there by 7:30.
2 Jane *sometimes watches* / *watches sometimes* TV after dinner, and she *often reads* / *reads often* a book before she goes to bed.
3 My father *goes always* / *always goes* to bed very early because he *is usually* / *usually is* tired by 10 o'clock.
4 I *often am* / *am often* at work before 9 o'clock, and I *don't finish usually* / *don't usually finish* work until 7 o'clock.

b Put the words in the correct order to make sentences. (Sometimes there is more than one possible answer.)

1 with their grandparents / lunch / usually / Sundays / they / have / on .
They usually have lunch with their grandparents on Sundays.
2 always / on / am / I / after my fitness class / tired / Fridays .
____
3 at / work / my manager / 7:30 / starts / in the morning / often .
____
4 on the weekends / together / never / dinner / has / his / family .
____
5 on Sundays / you / what time / do / go to bed / usually ?
____
6 gets / Paul / sometimes / on his math tests / 100% .
____

2 PRONUNCIATION Sentence stress

a 03.01 Listen to the sentences and check (✓) the correct stress markings.

1 a ☑ I **go** to the **gym** **twice** a **week**.
  b ☐ I go **to** the gym twice **a** week.
2 a ☐ **How** often **does** your brother **play** football?
  b ☐ How **often** does your brother play **foot**ball?
3 a ☐ Caroline eats **fruit** **every** **day**.
  b ☐ **Caroline** eats fruit every **day**.
4 a ☐ Do they **often** go to the Chi**nese** **res**taurant?
  b ☐ **Do** they often **go** to the **Chi**nese restaurant?
5 a ☐ We go on vacation **three** times a **year**.
  b ☐ We **go** on vaca**tion** three times **a** year.
6 a ☐ My brother **never** does any **ex**ercise.
  b ☐ My brother never **does** any exercise.

3 VOCABULARY Time expressions

a Miguel has a very busy schedule. Use the information in the chart to complete the sentences.

How often do you do these activities?	Sun	Mon	Tues	Wed	Thurs	Fri	Sat
1 go to school		✓	✓	✓	✓	✓	✓
2 study math			✓		✓		
3 play basketball		✓		✓			✓
4 go swimming	✓	✓	✓		✓		
5 watch TV	✓	✓	✓	✓	✓	✓	✓
6 visit your grandparents	✓						
7 have band practice		✓		✓		✓	
8 work as a waiter in the café						✓	✓

1 Miguel ___goes___ to school ___six times a___ week.
2 He ________ math ________ week.
3 He ________ basketball ________ week.
4 He ________ swimming ________ week.
5 He ________ TV ________ day.
6 He ________ his grandparents ________ week.
7 He ________ band practice ________ week.
8 He ________ as a waiter in the café ________ week.

4 VOCABULARY Common verbs

a Complete the sentences with the verbs in the box.

buy sells find decide help
~~try~~ prefer stay cost meet

1 Why don't we ___try___ the new café near the station?
2 When I go to Quito, I usually ________ with my friend, Jorge.
3 I ________ to go to the gym before I start work.
4 The new supermarket ________ Italian coffee. It's delicious!
5 I usually ________ a sandwich for lunch.
6 I don't like my job. I need to ________ a new one.
7 Can you ________ me carry the shopping bags?
8 I can't ________ which language to study – Spanish or Italian.
9 Why don't we ________ at the movie theater at 7:15?
10 How much does a cup of tea ________ in the new café?

3B IMAGINE YOU DON'T HAVE THE INTERNET

1 GRAMMAR *do, go, have*

a Underline the correct words to complete the sentences.

1 I <u>*have*</u> / *has* / *does have* a great new smartphone. It *have* / <u>*has*</u> / *does have* some amazing apps.
2 **A** *Do go* / *Do you goes* / *Do you go* out to eat every weekend?
B No, we *don't* / *doesn't* / *do*.
3 Sharon *do* / *does* / *doesn't* her homework after dinner.
4 I *go* / *do go* / *goes* to work at 7:00, and my husband *go* / *do go* / *goes* to work at 8:30.
5 She *has* / *have* / *do have* a fantastic new camera. It *has* /*have* / *do have* 20 megapixels!

b Complete the conversation with the words in the box.

have goes ~~do you have~~ do do you go
doesn't have (x2) does he have does don't

ADAM [1] <u>Do you have</u> a computer?
SAM Yes, I do. I [2]__________ a laptop. I [3]__________ most of my homework on my laptop. My brother often uses my laptop, too, because he [4]__________ a computer.
ADAM [5]__________ a tablet?
SAM Yes, he [6]__________, but he [7]__________ a keyboard for it. So sometimes he uses my laptop, and sometimes he [8]__________ to the library to use a computer.
ADAM [9]__________ to the library with him?
SAM No, I [10]__________. I usually work at home.

3 PRONUNCIATION Word stress

a 03.02 Listen and check (✓) the words with the correct stress marking.

1	a ☑ com<u>pu</u>ter		b ☐ compu<u>ter</u>	
2	a ☐ head<u>phones</u>		b ☐ <u>head</u>phones	
3	a ☐ tab<u>let</u>		b ☐ <u>tab</u>let	
4	a ☐ <u>smart</u>watch		b ☐ smart<u>watch</u>	
5	a ☐ key<u>board</u>		b ☐ <u>key</u>board	
6	a ☐ lap<u>top</u>		b ☐ <u>lap</u>top	
7	a ☐ <u>ca</u>mera		b ☐ came<u>ra</u>	
8	a ☐ prin<u>ter</u>		b ☐ <u>prin</u>ter	
9	a ☐ <u>spea</u>ker		b ☐ spea<u>ker</u>	
10	a ☐ smart<u>phone</u>		b ☐ <u>smart</u>phone	

2 VOCABULARY Technology

a Complete the crossword puzzle.

→ Across
5 You use <u>headphones</u> to listen to music on your MP3 player.
7 I can take a photo of you with the __________ on my cell phone.
8 If you want to see a paper copy of a document, you need to have a __________.
9 A __________ doesn't have a keyboard or a mouse. You only need to touch the screen.
10 You can use your __________ to call, text, or email your friends. You can also use the Internet, play games, and check maps.

↓ Down
1 A __________ is a small computer that you can carry with you.
2 When I want to listen to music with my friends, I connect my phone to a wireless __________.
3 I think the __________ on my laptop is very hard to use. It's really small and I've got big hands!
4 Some families have two or three __________ at home.
6 A __________ is a computer you wear on your wrist.

3C EVERYDAY ENGLISH
How about next Wednesday?

1 USEFUL LANGUAGE Making plans

a Complete the conversation with the words in the box.

let me see	you free	don't you	fine	I can't
that'd be	how about	great idea	~~don't we~~	

CHRIS Why [1] _don't we_ play tennis this weekend?
LUCY Tennis? Yeah, [2] ________ great!
CHRIS [3] ________ on Sunday afternoon?
LUCY Hmm, maybe. [4] ________. Oh, I'm sorry, [5] ________. I have plans to visit my grandmother on Sunday.
CHRIS Are [6] ________ on Saturday, then?
LUCY Yes, Saturday's [7] ________.
CHRIS Great. Why [8] ________ ask Tanya, too?
LUCY Yes, that's a [9] ________.

b ▶ 03.03 Listen and check.

c Put the conversation in the correct order.

- ☐ **LUKE** Hmm, maybe. Let me see. No, I'm sorry, I can't.
- [1] **TOM** Why don't we try that new Japanese restaurant this weekend?
- ☐ **TOM** Why don't you bring your sister, too?
- ☐ **LUKE** Yes, I'd love to. When are you free?
- ☐ **TOM** OK, no problem. Are you free on Saturday?
- ☐ **LUKE** I need to work late on Friday.
- ☐ **LUKE** Sure. That's a really good idea.
- ☐ **TOM** Great. See you on Saturday.
- ☐ **TOM** Oh, that's too bad. Why not?
- ☐ **LUKE** Yes, I am. Saturday's fine.
- ☐ **TOM** How about on Friday?

d ▶ 03.04 Listen and check.

2 PRONUNCIATION Main stress

a ▶ 03.05 Listen and check (✓) the stressed word in each sentence.

1 Why don't we see a movie?
  a ☐ see b ☑ movie
2 Yes, that's fine.
  a ☐ that's b ☐ fine
3 Do you want to get coffee after class?
  a ☐ coffee b ☐ class
4 Can I bring Jack?
  a ☐ bring b ☐ Jack
5 Here's your coffee, Valeria.
  a ☐ Here's b ☐ coffee
6 Yes, I'd love to.
  a ☐ love b ☐ to
7 That'd be great.
  a ☐ be b ☐ great
8 Why don't we try it?
  a ☐ Why b ☐ try

3D SKILLS FOR WRITING
Can you join us?

1 READING

a Read the emails and check (✓) the correct answers.

1 Luisa writes to Frida because she wants to…
- a ☐ tell Frida about her new apartment in Los Angeles.
- b ☐ stay with Frida in Guadalajara.
- c ☐ invite Frida to come to Los Angeles for her birthday.
- d ☐ invite Frida to her wedding.

2 Frida can't come because…
- a ☐ she needs to work.
- b ☐ her mom wants to visit her.
- c ☐ her sister is getting married.
- d ☐ she is on vacation that weekend.

Hi Frida,

How are you? I hope you like your new apartment in Guadalajara.

My birthday is next month, and I'd like to spend it with my closest friends. Would you like to come and stay with me in Los Angeles on June 15? I have an extra bedroom. I really hope you can come.

Love,

Luisa

Hi Luisa,

It's great to hear from you and thanks so much for the invitation. I'd love to come, but I have to go to a family wedding (for my sister, Eva) in Monterrey that weekend, so I can't go to Los Angeles. How about the weekend after that?

Have a great birthday and hope to see you soon.

Love,

Frida

b Read the emails again. Underline the correct words to complete the sentences.

1 Frida lives in *Los Angeles / Monterrey / Guadalajara*.
2 Luisa's birthday is in *May / June / July*.
3 If she comes to Los Angeles, Frida can stay *in a hotel / with Luisa / with her sister*.
4 Frida has a wedding in *Guadalajara / Los Angeles / Monterrey* when it's Luisa's birthday.
5 Frida would like to stay with Luisa on *June 15 / July 15 / June 22*.

2 WRITING SKILLS Inviting and replying

a Correct the mistakes in the conversation.

1 **MATEO** Hi, Clara. How you are?
Hi, Clara. How are you?
2 **CLARA** Hello, Mateo. Fine, thanks. How you are?
3 **MATEO** Great, thank.
4 **CLARA** Good. It's my birthday next Saturday. Would you like to join for dinner at my house?
5 **MATEO** Yes, I love to. It would be great to see you, Gabriel, and Sergio again.
6 **CLARA** Oh, good! And our barbecue is on the 18th. Would you like come?
7 **MATEO** I'd love to, but I afraid I can't. I have an important business trip to Quito that weekend, and I can't change it.
8 **CLARA** No problem. It OK.
9 **MATEO** I hope you all to have a great time at the barbecue. See you on Saturday.
10 **CLARA** Yeah, I really looking forward to it. Bye!

b 03.06 Listen and check.

3 WRITING

a Choose an event and write an invitation to a friend or family member. Use the information in the box. Remember to:

- start and finish the invitation with a greeting and an ending (e.g., *Hello, Love, …*)
- ask how they are
- tell them where and when the event is
- talk about where they can stay
- say you hope they can come.

A Summer Pool Party
When: July 23
Where: Your parents' house
Where people can stay: Two extra bedrooms

Housewarming Party*
When: *October 7*
Where: *Your new apartment*
Where people can stay: *Hotels downtown*

*a party when you invite friends to your new home

b Now imagine you are your friend or family member. You can't go to the event. Write a reply and say why you can't go. Remember to:

- start and finish the reply with a greeting and an ending (e.g., *Hello, Love, …*)
- say thank you for the invitation
- say why you can't go
- say you hope the party goes well.

UNIT 3
Reading and listening extension

1 READING

a Read the text. Use the words in the box to complete the summary of the text.

end	friendly	friends	~~magazine~~	often	questions

This is a page from a [1]__magazine__. First, it talks about [2]__________ and how important they are. Then there is a quiz. It asks [3]__________ about things you do. It wants to see how [4]__________ you are. It asks how [5]__________ you do different things. At the [6]__________, it tells you how friendly you are.

b Write your own quiz with questions about how often people do things. It can be about anything you like – types of food people eat, what they do to stay healthy, how they travel to work or school – anything you can think of! Here are some phrases you can use:

How often do you … ?
Once/twice a week
Once/twice a day
Three/four times a …

If you're so busy that you often forget about your friends, stop and think for a moment! Friends are very important. If you have good friends, there is always someone to talk to, someone to laugh with, and someone to help you with your problems. Life is more difficult for people who don't have friends.

Remember that it's not easy to make friends! If you want friends, you need to be friendly. Don't always wait for your friends to call you. Make sure you call them sometimes, too. If someone invites you to their house, invite them to your house next time. If they have problems, try to help them.

We can't choose our families, but we can choose our friends. If you're not friendly, people may not choose you!

So how friendly are you?
Take our quiz and find out!

HOW OFTEN DO YOU …

invite friends to your house?
a more than once a week
b once a week
c less than once a week

chat with your friends on the Internet?
a every day
b once or twice a week
c less than once a week

meet your friends (not at school or work)?
a more than twice a week
b once or twice a week
c less than once a week

have parties?
a three or four times a year or more
b once or twice a year
c less than once a year

send text messages to your friends?
a at least once an hour
b one to five times a day
c less than once a day

go on vacation with friends?
a once a year or more
b less than once a year
c never

Mostly "a" answers: You are very friendly. I want to be your friend! Make sure you leave time for work, too!

Mostly "b" answers: You have friends, but other things are important for you, too.

Mostly "c" answers: Your friends probably think you're not very interested in them. Try to be friendlier!

2 LISTENING

a 03.07 Listen to the conversation. <u>Underline</u> the correct words to complete the sentences.

1 Susie <u>*likes*</u> / *doesn't like* gadgets.
2 Adam *wants* / *doesn't want* many gadgets.
3 Susie *wants* / *doesn't want* to explain to Adam why smartwatches are useful.
4 Adam *wants* / *doesn't want* to meet Susie next week.

b Check (✓) the gadgets mentioned in the conversation.

☐ computer	☐ printer	☐ keyboard
☐ camera	☐ smartphone	☐ smartwatch
☐ headphones	☐ tablet	☐ speaker
☐ laptop		

c 03.07 Listen to the conversation again. Check (✓) the correct answers.

1 What does Susie show Adam at the beginning of their conversation?
   a ☐ a smartphone
   b ☑ a smartwatch
   c ☐ a speaker
2 What does Susie say she often uses her smartwatch for?
   a ☐ calling friends
   b ☐ going on the Internet
   c ☐ listening to music
3 Why does Adam say he needs a laptop?
   a ☐ to take photos
   b ☐ for his studies
   c ☐ to play games
4 Why does Susie invite Adam for a coffee?
   a ☐ to show him her tablet
   b ☐ to explain how useful a smartwatch is
   c ☐ to look at his laptop
5 When do Susie and Adam decide to meet?
   a ☐ next Monday
   b ☐ next month
   c ☐ next Friday
6 What does Susie say she can use to find the café?
   a ☐ her smartwatch
   b ☐ her laptop
   c ☐ her tablet

d Write about the gadgets you have and how you use them. Think about these questions:

- Which ones do you have? What do you use them for? Do you like them?
- Which ones don't you have? Why not? Would you like to have any of them?

Review and extension

1 GRAMMAR

Correct the sentences. (Sometimes there is more than one possible answer.)

1 My car have new speakers.
   My car has new speakers.
2 Look, I has the latest smartphone!
3 She don't have a good camera on her phone.
4 Do you has a laptop in your bag?
5 **A** Does they has apps on their phones?
   B Yes, they've.
6 We got a lot of friends in Ecuador.
7 **A** Do Julie have a big family?
   B No, she don't.
8 He have a new computer now.

2 VOCABULARY

Correct the sentences.

1 I usually go to soccer practice one time a week.
   I usually go to soccer practice once a week.
2 They go swimming everyday.
3 We study English three times the week.
4 My friends and I usually go to the movies about two times a month.
5 My sister goes to the gym once on the week.
6 My wife and I go on vacation three times at the year.

3 WORDPOWER *Prepositions of time*

<u>Underline</u> the correct words to complete the sentences.

1 He usually finishes work *in* / *on* / <u>*at*</u> 6 o'clock.
2 Julia's birthday is *on* / *in* / *at* April.
3 *At* / *In* / *On* the evening they sometimes watch TV.
4 The Great Lakes in the U.S. always freeze *in* / *on* / *at* the winter.
5 My parents often play tennis *at* / *on* / *in* Sundays.
6 *On* / *At* / *In* weekends I usually get up late.
7 That restaurant closes *at* / *in* / *on* midnight.
8 At my school, the first class starts *in* / *at* / *on* 8 o'clock.

REVIEW YOUR PROGRESS

Look again at Review Your Progress on p. 38 of the Student's Book. How well can you do these things now?
3 = very well 2 = well 1 = not so well

I CAN ...	
talk about routines	☐
talk about technology in my life	☐
make arrangements	☐
write an informal invitation.	☐

4A TRY SOME INTERESTING FOOD

1 GRAMMAR
Count and noncount nouns; *a / an, some, any*

a Underline the correct words to complete the sentences.

1 I need some *bread / breads* to make sandwiches.
2 Excuse me. Do you have any *carrot / carrots*?
3 The *pastas are / pasta is* really good at this restaurant.
4 I'd like *some lamb / a lamb*, please.
5 The *fruits are / fruit is* really fresh at this market.
6 You can buy fantastic *cheese / cheeses* at this market.
7 I love Mexican *food / foods* – I think it's the best in the world.
8 Can you buy me some *milks / milk* from the supermarket?

b Underline the correct words to complete the conversation. (Sometimes there is more than one possible answer.)

TIM We can make [1]*any / a / some* sandwiches for lunch.
RACHEL Good idea. Do we have [2]*any / some / a* bread?
TIM Yes, we do. We have [3]*any / some / a* really fresh bread. It's still warm!
RACHEL OK. Do we have [4]*any / some / a* turkey or chicken to put on it?
TIM Um, let me see. We don't have [5]*some / a / any* turkey, but we have [6]*some / a / any* chicken.
RACHEL Do we have [7]*a / some / any* cheese in the fridge?
TIM Yes, we have [8]*some / a / any* American cheese and [9]*any / a / some* Swiss cheese.
RACHEL OK. And what about vegetables? Do we have [10]*a / any / some*?
TIM Yes, we have [11]*a / some / any* mushrooms, and there's [12]*a / any / some* big tomato. But I'm afraid we don't have [13]*a / some / any* onions.
RACHEL OK. I can make [14]*some / a / any* cheese and tomato sandwich or [15]*a / any / some* chicken sandwich.

2 VOCABULARY Food

a Match the pictures with the words in the box.

chips salad pear lemon melon garlic burger grapes ~~chicken~~ cereal

1 chicken

2 ______

3 ______

4 ______

5 ______

6 ______

7 ______

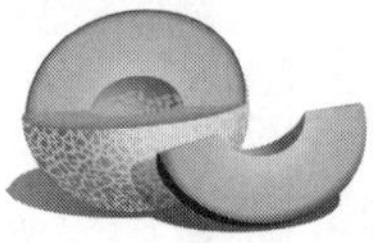
8 ______

9 ______

10 ______

b Complete the chart with the words in the box.

~~chicken~~ steak grape carrot mushroom burger melon onion pear lamb lemon garlic

Meat	Vegetables	Fruit
chicken		

3 PRONUNCIATION
Sound and spelling: *ea*

a 04.01 Listen and complete the chart with the words in the box.

~~see~~ hair meat pair great parent say bear need date meet hate air play sheep

/eɪ/ (e.g., *steak*)	/i/ (e.g., *bean*)	/eə/ (e.g., *pear*)
	see	

4B HOW MUCH CHOCOLATE DO YOU NEED?

1 GRAMMAR
Quantifiers: *much*, *many*, *a lot* (*of*)

a Put the words in the correct order to make sentences.

1 need / oranges / we / how / do / many ?
How many oranges do we need?
2 drinks / a / milk / of / she / lot / .
____
3 don't / much / sorry / have / money / I'm / I .
____
4 eat / brother / many / little / my / vegetables / doesn't .
____
5 day / you / fruit / every / do / much / eat / how ?
____
6 a / recipe / butter / need / for / little / this / we .
____
7 in / don't / afternoon / I / coffee / usually / the / much / drink .
____
8 few / for / can / tomatoes / you / a / buy / salad / the ?
____

b Complete the conversation with the words in the box.

many	much	a lot (x2)	a few	lot of
~~how much~~	a little	how many		

LUCA Hi, Nancy. I'm at the supermarket, but I forgot the shopping list. What do I need to buy?
NANCY Ha ha! No problem.
LUCA [1] *How much* milk do we need?
NANCY We need [2] ____________. Can you get two liters, please?
LUCA Sure! And [3] ____________ eggs?
NANCY Just [4] ____________. Just buy one carton of six.
LUCA OK. Do we need [5] ____________ vegetables?
NANCY Yes, we do. Buy a [6] ____________ vegetables. You know my mother's a vegetarian!
LUCA And do we need [7] ____________ cheese?
NANCY No, we still have [8] ____________ in the fridge, so don't buy any.
LUCA What about rice?
NANCY We only have [9] ____________ rice at home, so get one big bag.
LUCA OK, no problem.
NANCY OK, I think that's it. Thanks for going to the supermarket!

2 VOCABULARY Cooking

a Complete the food phrases with the words in the box.

roasted	jar	fried	bar	~~bag~~	package	bottle	grilled

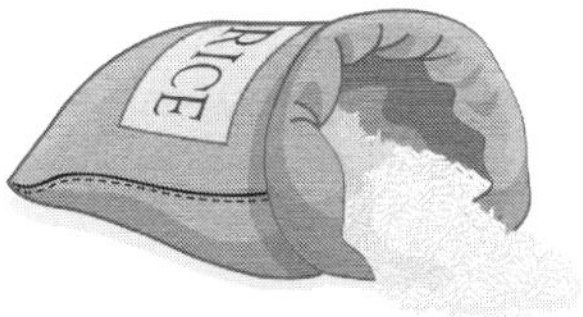

1 a *bag* of rice

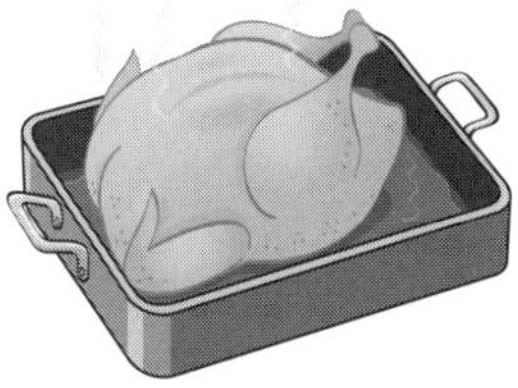

2 ____________ chicken

3 ____________ fish

4 ____________ eggs

5 a ____________ of jam

6 a ____________ of chocolate

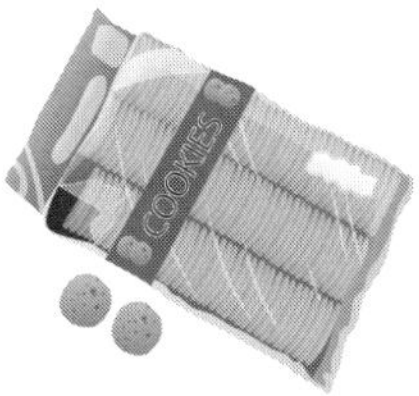

7 a ____________ of cookies

8 a ____________ of water

b 04.02 Listen and complete the sentences.

1 I'd like *boiled* potatoes, please.
2 I'd like ____________ fish, please.
3 I'd like ____________ vegetables, please.
4 I'd like a ____________ egg, please.
5 I'd like a ____________ of soda, please.
6 I'd like a ____________ of apples, please.
7 I'd like a ____________ of tomatoes, please.
8 I'd like a ____________ of chips, please.

4C EVERYDAY ENGLISH
Do we need a reservation?

1 USEFUL LANGUAGE
Arriving at and ordering a meal in a restaurant

a Complete the conversation with the words in the box.

maybe not | on the left | the name | can we have | this way | those two | prefer | ~~reservation~~ | for six | the one

HOST Good evening. Do you have a [1] *reservation* ?
PAUL Yes, we have a reservation [2]__________ people.
HOST Great! What's [3]__________?
PAUL Henderson.
HOST Yes, I see your name here.
PAUL [4]__________ a table outside, please?
HOST Yes, of course. [5]__________, please. [6]__________ over there are both free.
PAUL What do you think? [7]__________ on the right?
JENNY I'm not sure. What about the one [8]__________?
PAUL If you [9]__________. It's your birthday.
JENNY Well, [10]__________. This one's fine.

b 04.03 Listen and check.

c Check (✓) the correct sentences in the conversation. Correct the other sentences. (Sometimes there is more than one possible answer.)

1 ☐ **A** You are ready to order?
Are you ready to order?
2 ☐ **B** Yes, I think so.
3 ☐ **A** What do you like for your appetizer?
4 ☐ **B** I like the tossed salad, please.
5 ☐ **A** And for your entrée?
6 ☐ **B** I take the grilled steak.
7 ☐ **A** You like steamed vegetables with that?
8 ☐ **B** Yes, please.
9 ☐ **A** And in your appetizer, ma'am?
10 ☐ **C** I have the fried fish, please.
11 ☐ **A** Fried fish with lemon.
12 ☐ **C** Then I'd have the steak. No, wait. I'll have the lasagna.
13 ☐ **B** Oh, that's a good idea. Can I change my menu?
14 ☐ **A** Yes, of course.
15 ☐ **B** I'll eat the same. Vegetable lasagna for my entrée.

d 04.04 Listen and check.

2 PRONUNCIATION Word groups

a Match the phrases in the box to make sentences that people use in a restaurant.

Where would you like to sit
or do you need some more time?
~~and then the steak.~~
– inside or outside?
I'll have the soup
with some rice.
Can we have a table for four
~~I'd like the salad~~
by the window?
Would you like to order now
and the spaghetti for my entrée.
I'd like the lamb curry

	Word group 1	Word group 2
1	*I'd like the salad*	*and then the steak.*
2		
3		
4		
5		
6		

b 04.05 Listen and check.

c 04.06 Listen to the sentences and check (✓) the stressed words.

1 I'd like the tacos, please.
a ☑ tacos
b ☐ please
2 Can we have a table by the window?
a ☐ table
b ☐ window
3 I'd like the mushroom soup for my appetizer.
a ☐ mushroom soup
b ☐ appetizer
4 Would you like to order now?
a ☐ order
b ☐ now
5 I'll have the spaghetti for my entrée.
a ☐ spaghetti
b ☐ entrée
6 Where would you like to sit – outside?
a ☐ sit
b ☐ outside

4D SKILLS FOR WRITING

Next, decide on your menu

1 READING

a Read the recipe for Niçoise salad and check (✓) the correct answer.

1 ☐ This dish is for people who like a lot of meat.
2 ☐ This dish is for people who don't eat any meat or fish.
3 ☐ This dish is for people who like fish, vegetables, and eggs.
4 ☐ This dish is for people who don't like many vegetables.

b Read the recipe again. Are the sentences true or false?

1 You need to use fresh fish for this salad.
2 It takes less than an hour to make this salad.
3 You can add the eggs, potatoes, and beans to the salad when they're warm.
4 You put all the food together on the same plate.
5 You add the dressing last.

Niçoise Salad

Preparation time:
45 minutes

Ingredients:
For this recipe you need some fresh tuna fish (or a can of tuna), some potatoes, some tomatoes, some green beans, a large bag of lettuce, an onion, four eggs, and some black olives.

Instructions:

1 First, boil the eggs, potatoes, and green beans. Then put them in the refrigerator for one hour, or until they are cold.

2 Next, wash the lettuce and tomatoes and cut the onion into small pieces.

3 After that, put the lettuce on a large plate with the tuna, tomatoes, onion, potatoes, beans, and olives.

4 Finally, make a dressing with olive oil, vinegar, and mustard. Put it on the salad and mix everything together.

2 WRITING SKILLS
Making the order clear

a Read the recipe for a perfect omelet. Put the instructions in the correct order.

Spanish Omelet

Preparation time: about 45 minutes

Ingredients: For this recipe, you need six eggs, a large onion, 500 grams of potatoes, olive oil, salt and pepper.

Instructions:

☐ Next, cook all the ingredients together for about 10 minutes.

☐ Then fry the onions and potatoes in the olive oil for 30 minutes, or until the potatoes are soft.

☐ Finally, turn the omelet over and cook for 5 more minutes.

☐ After that, put the onions and potatoes into a large bowl with the eggs, salt, and pepper and mix everything together.

[1] First, cut the onion and potatoes into small pieces.

3 WRITING

a Look at the pictures of someone making a pizza. Use the information under the pictures to complete the recipe. Add your favorite pizza toppings. Remember to make the order clear (e.g., *First*, *After that*, …).

1 Mix: flour, water, oil

2 Make: pizza base

3 Add: tomato sauce, cheese

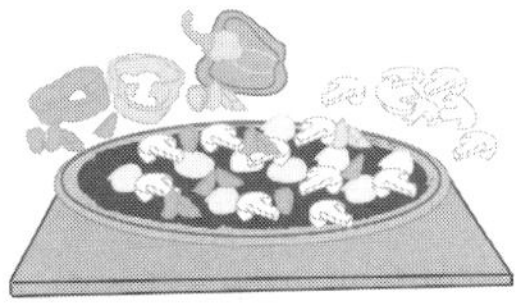

4 Add: toppings (e.g., mushrooms, peppers …)

5 Bake: 10 minutes

A ________ Pizza

Preparation time: ____________________

Ingredients: ____________________

Instructions:

First, ____________________

____

____

____

____

____

UNIT 4
Reading and listening extension

1 READING

a Read the magazine article. Complete each sentence with the correct paragraph number.

a Paragraph 4 talks about the fruit Rob grows.
b Paragraph ___ talks about how healthy it is to eat fruit and vegetables.
c Paragraph ___ talks about the vegetables Rob grows.
d Paragraph ___ talks about how good it is for children to see how we grow food.
e Paragraph ___ gives reasons to grow your own food.

b Read the article again. Are the sentences true or false?

1 It is expensive to grow your own vegetables.
2 You don't need a lot of space to grow a few vegetables.
3 Rob Green doesn't like growing vegetables because it's hard work.
4 He thinks his vegetables are better than the vegetables in the supermarkets.
5 He gets apples and oranges from his trees.
6 He bakes the apples he grows.
7 His children eat a lot of the strawberries.
8 His children think that vegetables always come from the supermarket.

c Write about the fruit and vegetables you eat. Think about these questions:

- What types of fruit and vegetables do you eat most often?
- What are your favorite vegetables?
- What is your favorite fruit?
- Do you think fruit and vegetables are expensive?
- Where do you get them from?
- Do you grow any fruit or vegetables (or do you know anyone who does)?

Are fresh fruit and vegetables too expensive?
Why not grow your own?

1 We all know that it's good for us to eat a lot of fresh fruit and vegetables. But it can be expensive, especially if you have a big family.

2 Why not grow your own? It's cheap, it's easy, and it's fun! You don't even need much space. Some containers in the window are enough to grow some food.

3 Rob Green has a vegetable garden at his house in Portland. He says, "It can be hard work sometimes, but I love it. I grow a lot of different vegetables, for example, carrots, onions, and beans. It saves me a lot of money, and the vegetables I grow are better than anything you can buy in the supermarkets."

4 His garden has an apple tree and a pear tree. The apples aren't very sweet, but he bakes them with brown sugar, and the family eats them for dessert with ice cream. Rob also grows strawberries, and he usually makes a few jars of jam each summer. "I'd like to make more," he says. "The only problem is that after the children see the strawberries, there aren't many left!"

5 Rob often cooks with his children, and he says that it's good for them to see where their food comes from, too. "Children need to know that food doesn't arrive at the supermarkets in packages."

2 LISTENING

a 04.07 Listen to the conversation. Check (✓) the correct words to complete the sentences.

1 Katie and Troy can't go out because …
  a [✓] of the snow.
  b [ ] they don't know where the supermarket is.
  c [ ] Troy wants to stay home and eat.
2 Troy is worried because …
  a [ ] he doesn't like bread.
  b [ ] he doesn't know how to cook.
  c [ ] they don't have much food.
3 Katie's not worried because …
  a [ ] she likes burgers.
  b [ ] she thinks she can cook a meal.
  c [ ] she wants to go out for a meal.
4 Katie's meal is very unusual because …
  a [ ] she only uses food she finds in the kitchen.
  b [ ] she likes making unusual food.
  c [ ] she only makes one dish.

b Complete the chart with the words in the box.

~~bread~~ eggs carrots cheese chocolate chips jam onions pasta rice yogurt

Katie and Troy have …	Katie and Troy don't have …
bread	

c 04.07 Listen to the conversation again. Put the sentences in the order they happen.

[ ] Troy doesn't like the sandwiches very much.
[ ] Troy doesn't think they can make a meal from the food they find.
[ ] For their appetizer, they have rice and cheese soup.
[1] Katie and Troy have to stay inside because of the snow.
[ ] Katie and Troy look in their kitchen to see what food they have.
[ ] For their entrée, they have carrot and fried onion sandwiches.
[ ] Katie says she will make a meal for them.
[ ] For dessert, they have boiled pasta and chocolate sauce.

d Think about the food in *your* kitchen. Write about an unusual meal you can make with the food you have. Use *much*, *a lot*, *many*, and *a little* to say how much of each food there is.

Review and extension

1 GRAMMAR

Correct the sentences.

1 I'd like any potatoes and any carrots, please.
  I'd like some potatoes and some carrots, please.
2 I'm sorry, I don't have a Swiss cheese this week.
3 Can I have some bag of rice, please?
4 Yes, we have any eggs in the fridge.
5 Can you buy a bread at the supermarket?
6 No, there aren't some mushrooms in the fridge.
7 We need a onion for the salad.
8 Do we have a milk?

2 VOCABULARY

Correct the sentences.

1 Can I have roasted kitchen and boiled potatoes, please?
  Can I have roasted chicken and boiled potatoes, please?
2 For my first dish, I'd like the mushroom soap.
3 Would you like braed with your salad?
4 I'll have lam curry and rice for my entrée.
5 Would you like some vedgetables with your steak?
6 I usually have serial with milk in the morning.
7 Do you eat yogurt with frute? It's delicious!
8 Would you like a cheese sanwhich?

3 WORDPOWER *like*

Match questions 1–6 with answers a–f.

1 [d] Would you like to have coffee with me?
2 [ ] What type of food do you like?
3 [ ] What would you like?
4 [ ] What's your sister like?
5 [ ] What kind of music does she like?
6 [ ] Is your sister like you?

a Yes, she is. We're both very tall.
b She likes rock, pop, and jazz.
c She's friendly and very popular.
d Yes, I'd love to.
e I like Italian food.
f I'd like a large pizza, please.

REVIEW YOUR PROGRESS

Look again at Review Your Progress on p. 48 of the Student's Book. How well can you do these things now?
3 = very well 2 = well 1 = not so well

I CAN …	
talk about the food I want	[ ]
talk about the food I eat every day	[ ]
order a meal at a restaurant	[ ]
write a blog about something I know how to do.	[ ]

5A THERE AREN'T ANY PARKS OR SQUARES

1 GRAMMAR *there is / there are*

a Underline the correct words to complete the conversation.

A [1]*Is there* / Are there / *There is* any good places to go in the evening?
B Yes, [2]*there is* / *it is* / *there are.* [3]*There is* / *There's* / *There are* some dance clubs and cafés.
A [4]*There is* / *Are there* / *Is there* any good restaurants?
B Yes, [5]*there are* / *there's* / *there is.* [6]*There are* / *There's* / *It's* a fantastic Italian restaurant in the town square.
A [7]*There is* / *There are* / *Is there* a theater?
B No, [8]*there is* / *there isn't* / *there aren't*, but [9]*there are* / *there's* / *there isn't* one in Springfield.
A What about interesting places to visit?
B Well, [10]*there's* / *there are* / *is there* an old castle, but [11]*there isn't* / *there are* / *there aren't* any museums or art galleries.
A [12]*Are there* / *Is there* / *There is* a subway?
B No, but we have a good bus system.

b Put the words in the correct order to make sentences.

1 **A** your town / there / in / nice restaurants / are / any ?
Are there any nice restaurants in your town?
B there / yes, / are .
____
2 **A** beautiful park / there / downtown / is / a ?
____
B is / yes, / there .
____
3 near / there / subway station / a / isn't / my house .
____
4 near / stores / any / there / my office / aren't .
____
5 the station / there / near / cheap hotels / are / some .
____
6 my apartment building / there's / near / new café / a .
____
7 **A** downtown / any / there / are / interesting buildings ?
____
B aren't / no, / there .
____

2 VOCABULARY Places in a city

a Write the names of the places in a city under the pictures.

1 concert hall

2 ______________

3 ______________

4 ______________

5 ______________

6 ______________

b Complete the sentences with the words in the box.

street	post office	fitness center	buildings
police station	theater	stadium	~~restaurant~~

1 The pizzas at the new Italian restaurant are amazing!
2 They have Shakespeare's *Romeo and Juliet* at our local ______________.
3 There are a lot of houses on my ______________, and there are also a few stores and cafés.
4 There's a soccer game at the ______________.
5 You can buy stamps for your postcards at the ______________.
6 There are a lot of beautiful ______________ in our town. The concert hall and museum are amazing!
7 There is a fantastic pool at our ______________.
8 If someone takes your cell phone, you need to go to the ______________.

3 PRONUNCIATION
Sound and spelling: /b/ and /p/

a 05.01 Listen and underline the correct words.

1 big / pig
2 put / but
3 buy / pie
4 bear / pear
5 part / Bart
6 be / pea

5B WHOSE COUCH IS THAT?

1 GRAMMAR Possessive pronouns and possessive *'s*

a Choose the correct words to complete the sentences.

1 This isn't *Alans' car* / *the Alan car* / *<u>Alan's car</u>*. It's *my* / *<u>mine</u>* / *the mine*.
2 *Our* / *Ours* / *The our* parents live in downtown Houston.
3 No, this isn't *the my* / *my* / *mine* dog. It's *their* / *theirs* / *they're*.
4 Sarah is *Matthew's sister* / *the sister Matthew* / *Matthews sister*. *Her* / *Hers* / *His* boyfriend's French.
5 *Who's* / *Whose* / *Who* phone is this? Is it *the your* / *your* / *yours*?
6 *Jim and Anna* / *The Jim and Annas'* / *Jim and Anna's* apartment has two large bedrooms.

b Find the mistakes in the words in **bold** and rewrite the sentences.

1 **A** **Who's** apartment is this?
Whose apartment is this?
B It's **Monicas**.
______
2 I gave my car to my parents. It's **their** now.
______
3 **Hers** sister, Christina, lives with her. **Their** identical twins.
______
4 They have a cat, but **its** not **there's**. **Its** their **brothers** cat. **It's** name's Brandy.
______
5 **Monicas** bedroom is pretty big, but **Christinas'** bedroom is very small.
______
6 **A** **Who's** furniture is this?
______
B Monica says that the couch is **her**, but Christina says **its** her **brother**.
______
7 **There** brother has a new couch. **Its** really comfortable!
______

2 VOCABULARY Furniture

a Complete the crossword puzzle with the words in the box.

armchair bookcase couch curtains dresser lamp mirror nightstand sink stove wardrobe washing machine

→ Across
3 You can wash the plates and cups in the ______.
4 You need to turn on the ______ when it gets dark.
7 Three people can sit on that big ______ to watch TV.
10 You can do your laundry in the ______.
11 Is there a ______ in the kitchen so I can cook my dinner?
12 After you fold your sweaters, shirts, and pants, put them in this ______.

↓ Down
1 I have a clock on the <u>nightstand</u> next to my bed.
2 I don't have a closet. I hang my shirts and sweaters in the ______.
5 Close your ______ before you go to bed at night.
6 You can put all of your books on that ______ in the living room.
8 I like to sit in my favorite ______ when I read.
9 I always look in the ______ when I brush my teeth or put on makeup.

3 PRONUNCIATION Sound and spelling: vowels before *r*

a 05.02 Look at the words and listen to the pronunciation of the letters in **bold**. Which words have the same sounds?

~~h**er**~~ b**or**ing f**ur**niture airp**or**t dess**er**t d**oor** c**ur**tains y**our** c**er**tain w**ar**drobe

/ɜr/ (e.g., *shirt*)	/ɔr/ (e.g., *short*)
her	

5C EVERYDAY ENGLISH
Is there a theater near here?

1 USEFUL LANGUAGE
Asking for and giving directions

a Put the conversation in the correct order.

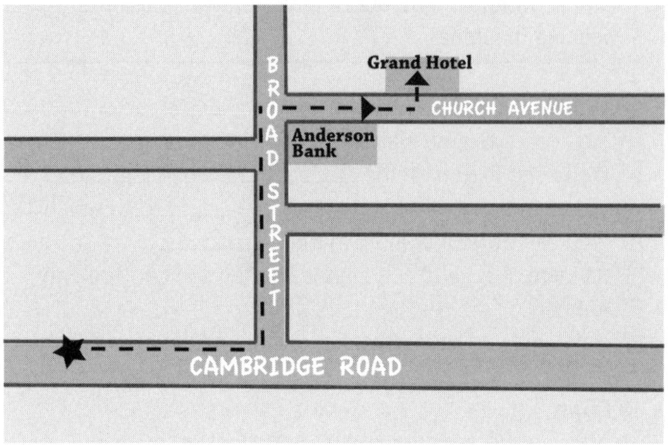

- ☐ So, go straight, then turn left onto Broad Street?
- ☐ Yes, then go down Church Avenue for about 100 meters. The hotel is on your left.
- 1 Excuse me. Can you tell me how to get to the Grand Hotel, please?
- ☐ Yes, that's right. Then go straight on Broad Street until you come to Anderson Bank. Then turn right onto Church Avenue.
- ☐ Great. Thanks very much.
- ☐ Yes, of course. Go straight for about 200 meters, then turn left onto Broad Street.
- ☐ So, that's right onto Church Avenue after the bank?

b 05.03 Listen and check.

c Put the words in the correct order to make sentences.

1 until / go / you come / on / straight / your / to / a subway station / left .
Go straight until you come to a subway station on your left.

2 turn left / and go down / the movie theater / at / for 250 meters / Cedar Road.

____

3 please / you / can / how / get / us / tell / to / the station / to ?

____

4 down / for 100 meters, / go / High Street / right / your / and the concert hall / is / on .

____

5 is / stop / a / here / bus / near / there ?

____

6 straight / for 250 meters, / go / right / then turn / Park Street / onto .

____

7 it's / the / corner / next / on / the bank / to .

____

8 I / to / do / the train station / how / from here / get ?

____

d 05.04 Listen and check.

2 PRONUNCIATION Sentence stress

a 05.05 Listen and check (✓) the stressed word in each sentence.

1 Go down Ninth Street.
a ☐ go
b ☑ Ninth

2 Go straight until you come to the hospital.
a ☐ come
b ☐ hospital

3 Can you tell me how to get to the swimming pool, please?
a ☐ swimming pool
b ☐ please

4 Go straight for about 300 meters.
a ☐ go
b ☐ straight

5 Turn right onto Carlisle Avenue.
a ☐ turn
b ☐ right

6 The fitness center is on the left.
a ☐ on
b ☐ left

7 Is there a bank near here?
a ☐ bank
b ☐ here

8 Go straight for about 150 meters.
a ☐ 150
b ☐ meters

5D SKILLS FOR WRITING
It isn't very exciting, but it's a nice place to live

1 READING

a Jessica wants to sell her apartment. Read her online ad and check (✓) the pictures that she talks about.

Apartment For Sale

Hi, I'm Jessica, and I need to sell my apartment in Los Angeles because I have a new job in San Diego.

This large apartment is about a mile from Hollywood, and there's a bus stop in front of the building. There is a big living room with a private balcony. You can see a beautiful view of the Hollywood Hills. The bathroom has a large shower. The sink and stove in the kitchen are new. There's one big bedroom with a big window, so you need curtains. I don't want to bring my couch or bookcases with me, so I can sell them to you. The neighborhood is busy during the day and very quiet at night. The neighbors don't make any noise.

Text me at 555-555-1234 if you want to see the apartment. Thanks!

Posted 1 week ago

b Read the online ad again. Are the sentences true or false?

1 The apartment is far from Hollywood.
2 The bus stop is near Jessica's apartment.
3 You can't see anything nice from the balcony.
4 Jessica wants to sell some furniture with the apartment.
5 It's difficult to sleep at night in Jessica's neighborhood.

2 WRITING SKILLS
Linking ideas with *and*, *but*, and *so*

a Underline the best words to complete the sentences.

1 Jeff doesn't have a lot of furniture, *and* / *but* / *so* his apartment doesn't look empty.
2 I live near a bus stop, *so* / *but* / *and* I don't need to drive.
3 Simon's house is next to the park, *so* / *and* / *but* there's a small river there as well.
4 We have a really big TV in our living room, *so* / *and* / *but* it doesn't work.
5 My neighbors have eight children, *but* / *and* / *so* it's always very noisy.
6 There's a great market near my house, *so* / *but* / *and* it's easy to get fresh fruit and vegetables.

3 WRITING

a Imagine you want to sell your house or apartment. Write an online ad. Remember to:

- say why you want to sell your apartment
- say where it is in the city or town
- say how many rooms it has and what they are
- say what furniture you also want to sell
- talk about the neighborhood
- use adjectives (e.g., *big*, *modern*, *quiet*, ...)
- use *and*, *but*, and *so* when possible.

UNIT 5
Reading and listening extension

1 READING

From: Carrie

To: Jen

Re: Long time, no see!

Hi Jen!

How are you? I'll be in the city next Friday. If you're not busy, let's go out to eat. I want to try the new Chinese restaurant downtown. What do you think?

You have to see Romina's new apartment soon – it's so cool! It's in that really tall building near the library, and the view from her bedroom window is amazing, especially at night. You can see the whole city.

It's not very big, but there's a large mirror on the living room wall and that makes it look bigger. She has some beautiful furniture and a big, red sofa from her aunt's house. It's so comfortable – perfect for when you want to chat all evening!

The kitchen is a great space too. It's very modern. It's great for Romina because she's a fantastic cook.

There are two bedrooms, so her sister can stay with her when she wants. Do you know Romina's sister? She's an actor, and she usually works at the theater here once or twice a year.

Next time she comes, we can all go out together if you want.

Anyway, I hope you're well, and let me know about Friday!

Love,

Carrie

a Read Carrie's email to Jen. Are the sentences true or false?

1 Jen often goes to Romina's apartment.
2 Carrie likes Romina's apartment.
3 Romina's sister lives with her.

b Read the email again. Match 1–8 with a–h to make sentences.

1 Carrie wants to go	a city from Romina's bedroom.
2 Romina's apartment is in	b in Romina's apartment.
3 You can see the whole	c a tall building.
4 A large mirror makes	d is very modern.
5 Romina has her aunt's	e Romina's living room look big.
6 Romina's kitchen	f red sofa in her living room.
7 There are two bedrooms	g stays in her apartment.
8 Romina's sister sometimes	h to a Chinese restaurant.

c Think about an apartment or house where you would like to live. Write a description of the rooms and the furniture.

2 LISTENING

a 05.06 Listen to the conversation. Complete the sentences with the words in the box.

find get ~~meet~~ starts

1 Dan and Jack agree to meet outside a restaurant.
2 Jack calls Dan because he can't ____________ him.
3 Jack tells Dan how to ____________ to the Flame & Grill restaurant.
4 Dan ____________ at the wrong subway station.

b Check (✓) the places you hear in the conversation.

☑ restaurant	☐ concert hall
☐ square	☐ bridge
☐ café	☐ river
☐ post office	☐ castle
☐ police station	☐ theater

c 05.06 Listen again. Underline the correct words to complete the sentences about the conversation.

1 Dan and Jack both wait outside a *post office* / *restaurant* / *river*.
2 The Flame & Grill restaurant is near *Main Street* / *the theater* / *the river*.
3 Jack tells Dan to turn right at the *church* / *bridge* / *post office*.
4 Jack tells Dan the restaurant is *on his left* / *straight ahead* / *on his right*.
5 Dan tells Jack that he can't turn right because there is no *road* / *river* / *post office*.
6 Dan tells Jack that he can see a *river* / *theater* / *bridge* on his right.

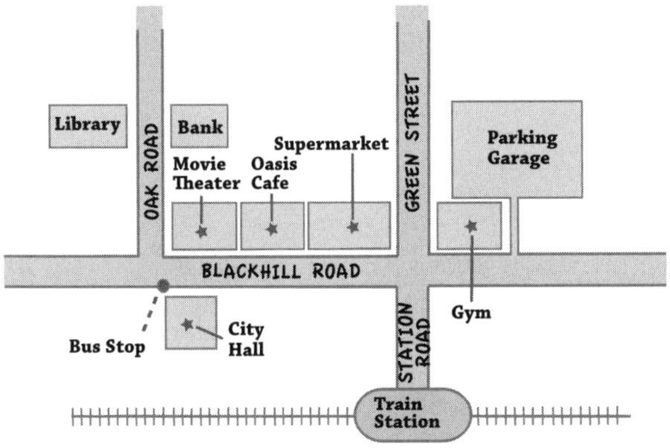

d Write a conversation between two people asking for and giving directions to places in your city or town. You can use these phrases:

Can you tell me how to get to … ?
Turn right/left.
Go straight.
It's on your right/left.
Go down ____________ *Street.*

Review and extension

1 GRAMMAR

Correct the sentences.

1 This isn't your phone. It's my.
This isn't your phone. It's mine.
2 My parent's apartment is downtown.
3 This isn't your bike. It's her.
4 My room number is 127. It's next to your.
5 Matt and Nick teacher is Argentinian.
6 Yours car is so fast!
7 This isn't our bus. It's their.
8 The phone my brother is new.

2 VOCABULARY

Correct the sentences.

1 There's a fantastic gym near my house.
There's a fantastic gym near my house.
2 The station subway is 100 meters after the bridge.
3 I don't go very downtown often.
4 My favorite resturaunt is called Green HIll.
5 There are a lot of beautiful old bildings in my town.
6 There is a nice parck near where I live.
7 I never go to the teater on the weekends.
8 The station police is across from City Hall.

3 WORDPOWER Prepositions of place

Look at the map on the left and complete the sentences with the words in the box.

in front of ~~next to~~ across from behind at the end between in on the corner on

1 The movie theater is next to the Oasis Café.
2 The bank is ________ Oak Road, ________ the library.
3 The train station is ________ of Station Road.
4 The bus stop is ________ City Hall.
5 The parking garage is on Blackhill Road, ________ the gym.
6 The gym is ________ of Blackhill Road and Green Street.
7 The Oasis Café is ________ the movie theater and the supermarket.
8 City Hall is ________ Blackhill Road.

REVIEW YOUR PROGRESS

Look again at Review Your Progress on p. 58 of the Student's Book. How well can you do these things now?
3 = very well 2 = well 1 = not so well

I CAN …	
talk about towns	☐
describe rooms and furniture in my home	☐
ask for and give directions	☐
write a description of my neighborhood.	☐

6A SHE WAS A DOCTOR

1 VOCABULARY Family

a Match the people in the family tree with the words in the box.

cousin mother sister aunt grandfather
brother uncle grandmother father

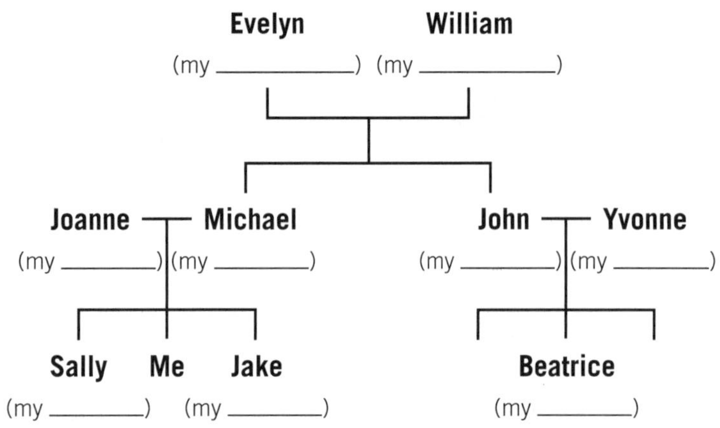

b Underline the correct words to complete the sentences.

1 My aunt and uncle's children are my *brothers* / *cousins* / *parents*.
2 My *cousins* / *grandchildren* / *grandparents* got married in 1970, and my father was born in 1972.
3 My aunt met my *grandfather* / *uncle* / *sister* in college, and they got married in 1993.
4 My uncle David's my mother's *brother* / *sister* / *cousin*.
5 My father has two sisters, Sarah and Michelle. They are my *grandmothers* / *aunts* / *cousins*.
6 Joe has one brother and two *parents* / *sisters* / *uncles*, Jenna and Caitlyn.

2 GRAMMAR Simple past: *be*

a Underline the correct words to complete the sentences.

1 **A** Where *are* / *were* / *was* you last night?
B I *am* / *were* / *was* at my grandparents' house.
2 **A** *Were* / *Are* / *Was* you with your brother?
B No, I *'m not* / *weren't* / *wasn't*.
3 My sister *were* / *was* / *wasn't* sick last week, so she *was* / *weren't* / *wasn't* at school.
4 My father *were* / *wasn't* / *weren't* in college in the 1970s. He *were* / *weren't* / *was* in college from 1989 to 1993.
5 **A** *Were* / *Was* / *Wasn't* your grandparents alive during the first moon landing?
B Yes, they *was* / *weren't* / *were*. My grandfather *were* / *was* / *is* born in 1960.
6 My sister and I *are* / *was* / *were* born in 1997.

b Complete the sentences with *was*, *were*, *wasn't*, or *weren't*.

1 He ___wasn't___ at work yesterday. He ___was___ on vacation in Las Vegas.
2 **A** ________ you in the U.S. when you got married?
B Yes, we ________.
3 They ________ here last night because they ________ at the hospital.
4 **A** Where ________ you born?
B I ________ born in Chicago.
5 **A** ________ your grandparents born in the U.S.?
B No, they ________. They ________ born in Brazil.
6 It ________ my mother's birthday yesterday.

3 PRONUNCIATION Sentence stress

a 06.01 Listen to the sentences. Are the words in **bold** stressed? Check (✓) *Yes* or *No*.

	Yes	No
1 My mother **was** a terrible student.	☐	✓
2 "Was he at **work** today?" "No, he **wasn't**."	☐	☐
3 Were you at the **party**?	☐	☐
4 We were **good friends**.	☐	☐
5 Peter **was** an engineer.	☐	☐
6 "**Was** he married?" "Yes, **he** was."	☐	☐

4 VOCABULARY Years and dates

a 06.02 Listen and check (✓) the correct dates.

1 a ☐ one thousand, nine hundred and sixty-eight
b ✓ nineteen sixty-eight
2 a ☐ twenty fifteen
b ☐ two thousand and fifteen
3 a ☐ nineteen thirty-nine
b ☐ one thousand, nine hundred and thirty-nine
4 a ☐ two thousand and six
b ☐ twenty oh six
5 a ☐ two thousand and twenty
b ☐ twenty twenty
6 a ☐ one thousand, four hundred and ninety-two
b ☐ fourteen ninety-two

6B I PLAYED ANYTHING AND EVERYTHING

1 GRAMMAR Simple past: affirmative

a Complete the text with the simple past forms of the verbs in parentheses.

Stan Lee [1]__________ (be) an American comic book writer. He [2]__________ (be born) in 1922 in New York City. He [3]__________ (have) one younger brother, Larry. As a boy, Lee [4]__________ (like) writing. In high school, he [5]__________ (enter) a weekly writing competition by a popular newspaper. Lee [6]__________ (win) the competition three weeks in a row. The newspaper [7]__________ (tell) him to become a professional writer. In 1942, Lee [8]__________ (join) the U.S. Army. While in the army, Lee [9]__________(write) one story a week for a comic book company. In the 1960s, Lee [10]__________ (help) create the Fantastic Four for Marvel Comics. The characters [11]__________ (be) so popular that Marvel Comics [12]__________ (ask) Lee to help create more characters and stories. Lee [13]__________ (become) famous for helping to create such characters as the Hulk, Thor, Iron Man, the X-Men, Daredevil, Doctor Strange, and Spider-Man. Lee [14]__________ (die) on November 12, 2018. He [15]__________ (receive) many awards during his lifetime.

b Underline the correct words to complete the sentences.

1 Andrew *meeted* / *met* / *metted* Laura when they *were* / *was* / *been* in college together.
2 The taxi *stopped* / *stoped* / *stopt* in front of the train station, and she *gived* / *gaved* / *gave* the driver $20.
3 He *were* / *was* / *am* born in 1942 and *died* / *die* / *dyed* in 2021.
4 When they *find* / *finded* / *found* the backpack in the park, they *taked* / *took* / *taken* it to the police station.
5 Last year, my brother *goed* / *was* / *went* to Las Vegas for a vacation. It's a really expensive place to visit. He *spent* / *spended* / *spented* over $2,000 in three days!
6 My mother *maked* / *maid* / *made* a big birthday cake for my brother yesterday, and we *eated* / *ate* / *ated* three pieces each!
7 My sister *playd* / *plaied* / *played* the piano very well when she was eight, and my parents *bought* / *buyed* / *buied* her a guitar when she was fifteen.
8 Elizabeth *workt* / *worked* / *walked* hard as a college student and then *getted* / *gotted* / *got* a fantastic job in Boston.

2 VOCABULARY Simple past irregular verbs

a Complete the sentences with the simple past forms of the verbs in the box.

go ~~eat~~ give read bring buy
think ~~make~~ have cost get come

1 Last night, she __made__ us a wonderful chicken soup. Sorry, there isn't any for you today because we __ate__ it all.
2 My uncle __________ a car last week. It __________ $8,000.
3 We __________ to an Italian restaurant last night and __________ some fantastic dishes!
4 She __________ to my house for dinner on Saturday and __________ her new boyfriend with her.
5 I __________ that new book about Leonardo Da Vinci over the weekend. I __________ it was really interesting.
6 I __________ some nice chocolates for my birthday. My friend Alison __________ them to me.

3 PRONUNCIATION *-ed* endings

a 06.03 Listen to the simple past verbs. Do they have an extra syllable? Check (✓) the correct box.

	No extra syllable: /t/ or /d/	Extra syllable: /əd/
1 closed	✓	
2 waited		
3 decided		
4 arrived		
5 loved		
6 studied		
7 visited		
8 opened		
9 started		
10 worked		

6C EVERYDAY ENGLISH

Can he call you back?

1 USEFUL LANGUAGE

Leaving a voicemail message and asking for someone on the phone

a Complete the conversation with the words in the box.

a minute   Ian Smith's office   ~~leave~~   's not here   back soon   there   it's   can he   ~~right now~~   on my cell   I'll tell   ~~this is~~   it's me   call me back

CONVERSATION 1

IAN Hello, 1 ___this is___ Ian Smith. I'm not here 2 ___right now___. Please 3 ___leave___ me a message.

ABBY Hi, Ian. Can you 4 ___________? You can call me at my work number or 5 ___________.

CONVERSATION 2

DAVID Hello. 6 ___________.

ABBY Oh, hello. Is Ian 7 ___________?

DAVID Sorry, he 8 ___________ right now. He's in a meeting.

ABBY That's OK. 9 ___________ his sister, Abby. 10 ___________ call me back?

DAVID OK, 11 ___________ him. He'll be 12 ___________. Oh, just 13 ___________. Here he comes now ... Ian, it's Abby.

IAN Hi, Abby. 14 ___________.

ABBY Hello, Ian. Finally!

b 06.04 Listen and check.

c Put the words in the correct order to make sentences.

1 me / leave / please / a message .
Please leave me a message.

2 this afternoon / back / can you / call me ?
____

3 can / wait / you / a minute ?
____

4 my cell / call me / on / you can / at work / or .
____

5 right now / I'm not / here .
____

6 here / right now / sorry, / she's not .
____

d 06.05 Listen and check.

2 PRONUNCIATION

Sound and spelling: *a*

a 06.06 Listen to the words with the *a* sounds in **bold**. Then complete the chart with the words in the box.

~~fall~~   d**a**te   cott**a**ge   **a**m   c**a**ke   langu**a**ge   dr**a**w   h**a**ppy   w**a**lk   c**a**t   man**a**ge   em**a**il   b**a**ll   m**a**n   n**a**me

/æ/ (e.g., *thanks*)	/ɔ/ (e.g., *call*)	/ɪ/ (e.g., *message*)	/eɪ/ (e.g., *later*)
	fall		

6D SKILLS FOR WRITING
Five months later, we got married

1 READING

a Read about Marco Morales and check (✓) the one wrong answer.

1 ☐ Marco wasn't born in the U.S.
2 ☐ His wife's name is Ruby.
3 ☐ He has two children.
4 ☐ They live in Arizona.

b Read about Marco Morales again. Are the sentences true or false?

1 Marco's family moved to Arizona in 1982.
2 He graduated when he was sixteen years old.
3 His first job was in a bank in Memphis.
4 Mason was born in 2015.
5 In 2016, Marco and his family left the U.S.

Marco was born in El Salvador in 1978. When he was four years old, his family moved to Arizona in the U.S. because his father got a job as an engineer in Phoenix. Marco went to school in Scottsdale. He graduated in 1996 and went to college in Florida. He studied Economics there. He graduated from college in 2000 and got his first job with a big bank in Miami. In 2005, he met Ruby, and they got married in 2009. Six years later, their first child, Mason, was born. In 2016, Marco and Ruby moved to Mexico City. Marco became the vice president of a bank there, and Ruby got a job as a teacher at an international school. Their daughter, Lydia, was born in 2017.

2 WRITING SKILLS
Linking ideas in the past

a Complete the paragraph with the words in the box. Use Sarah's timeline to help you.

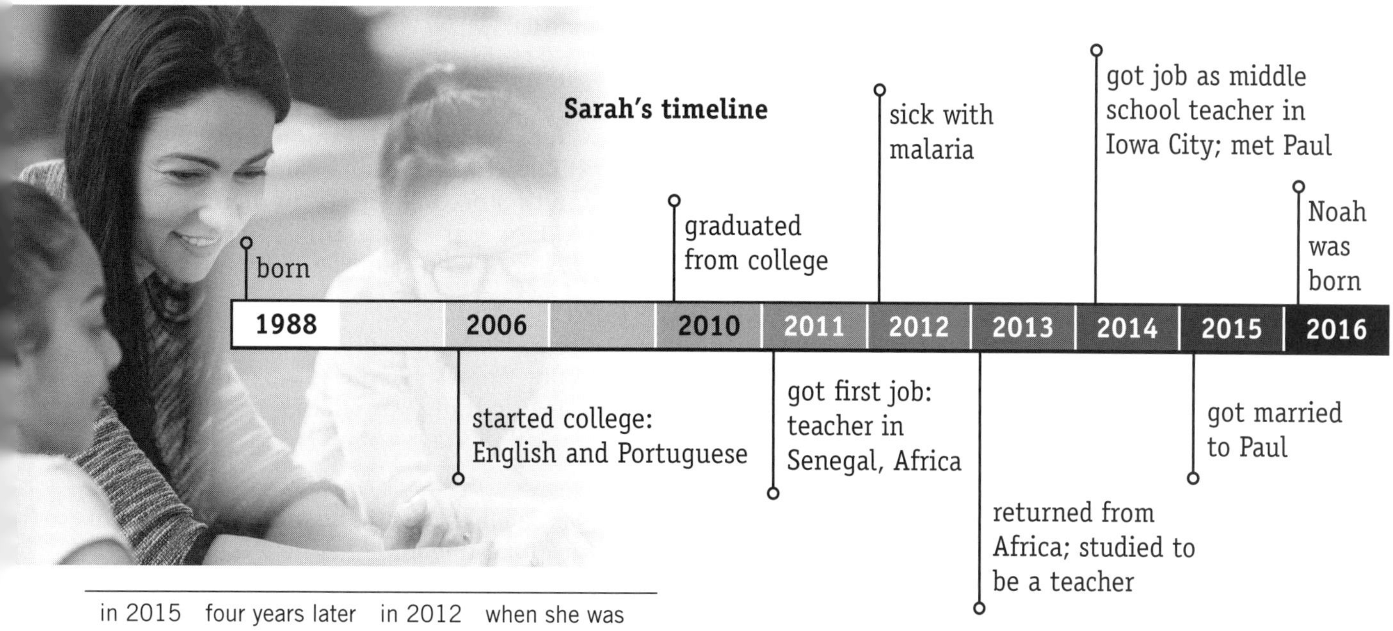

in 2015 four years later in 2012 when she was in 2011 a year later ~~she was 18~~ in 2013 when in 2014

Sarah was born in Mississippi in 1988. When [1] *she was 18*, Sarah went to college in Wisconsin, where she studied English and Portuguese. [2]__________ she graduated from college, and [3]__________ she got her first job in Africa. [4]__________ in Senegal, she worked as an English teacher. [5]__________ she was sick with malaria for three months. [6]__________ she returned to the U.S. and went back to school to become a teacher. [7]__________ she got a job at a school in Iowa City. [8]__________ she was in Iowa City, she met her husband, Paul. [9]__________ they got married, and [10]__________ their first child, Noah, was born.

3 WRITING

a Write the life story of a famous person. Use linking phrases in the story. Think about:

- when/where they were born
- where/what they studied
- what jobs they did in the past and now
- where they lived in the past and now
- their family (parents, husband/wife, children).

UNIT 6
Reading and listening extension

1 READING

a Read the text. Complete each sentence with the correct paragraph number.

1 Paragraph _5_ talks about the good idea Nina's mom had.
2 Paragraph ___ says that her grandmother was worried about possible problems.
3 Paragraph ___ talks about a visit from her dad's cousin.
4 Paragraph ___ says that they knew her dad wasn't happy.
5 Paragraph ___ describes where Nina lived when she was a child.

b Read the text again and check (✓) the best endings for the sentences.

1 Nina's mom went to live on the farm …
 a ☐ after Nina was born.
 b ☑ after she got married to Nina's dad.
 c ☐ when she was a child.

2 Nina's mom …
 a ☐ liked her husband's mother.
 b ☐ wanted a different house.
 c ☐ didn't like her husband's mother.

3 Nina knew that her dad …
 a ☐ was happy.
 b ☐ wanted a different job.
 c ☐ wasn't happy.

4 Nina's dad was unhappy when his cousin came because …
 a ☐ he didn't like his cousin.
 b ☐ he felt sick.
 c ☐ he didn't like being a farmer.

5 Nina's Mom …
 a ☐ wanted to work on the farm.
 b ☐ wanted to become a teacher.
 c ☐ didn't want to work on the farm.

6 In the end, Nina's dad was happy because …
 a ☐ his cousin went away.
 b ☐ his children liked the farm.
 c ☐ he changed his job.

c Write about two people in your family who are older than you: your parents, your grandparents, or two other people.

- Describe their lives when you were a small child.
- Did they live near you? In the same house? Far away from you?
- What were their jobs? Did they like them? Did they change jobs?

1 My family lived on a farm. It was my grandfather's farm. He and my dad worked together, and when Mom and Dad got married, Mom lived there, too. Soon they had three children – me and my brothers. It was a good place for children to grow up.

2 Mom's mother said it was a mistake to live with Dad's parents. She said that Mom and Dad needed a house of their own. But Mom liked it on the farm, and she and my grandmother became good friends.

3 So my grandparents weren't a problem. Mom was happy, and my brothers and I were happy. The problem was my dad. He said that everything was OK, but we all knew that something was wrong.

4 One day, my dad's cousin came to visit. He was an engineer, and he told all of us about his interesting job. After he left, my dad looked really unhappy. That night, my mom asked him again what was wrong, and he told her. He hated the farm. He wanted to change his job, but he knew how important the farm was to his father. "I don't know what to do," he said.

5 Then my mom thought of a plan. "I love the farm," she said. "I can be the farmer in the family! You can get a different job, and your parents can keep the farm." So that's what they did. My mom became a farmer, my grandmother looked after us, and my dad went to college and became a teacher. After that, everyone was happy!

2 LISTENING

a 06.07 Listen to the conversation. Use the words in the box to make three sentences about the conversation.

a lot   and uncle   brothers or sisters   have any   love children   Maria doesn't   Maria has   Maria's parents   of cousins

b 06.07 Listen to the conversation again and complete the sentences.

1 Maria's cousins are all _girls_.
2 Maria's cousin Abigail has a ______ named Brooke.
3 Maria's cousin Amelia is Brooke's ______.
4 Maria's aunt and ______ always wanted to have a big family.
5 The cousins live in a big ______.
6 When she was young, Maria ______ a lot of time with her cousins.
7 Maria and her parents ______ near the cousins.
8 Maria's dad didn't ______ lots of children.

c Write about your brothers, sisters, and cousins (or friends you have known for a long time). Remember to say:

- how many brothers, sisters, and cousins you have
- how old they are
- how much time you spent with them when you were young and what you did together
- how much time you spend with them now
- what they are like and what they do now
- any other interesting things about them.

Review and extension

1 GRAMMAR

Correct the sentences.

1 The weather were terrible when we was in New York.
The weather was terrible when we were in New York.
2 I payed for the meal with my credit card.
3 He eated all his vegetables.
4 They really enjoied the movie.
5 Was you at work yesterday?
6 The ticket were very expensive. It costs $100!

2 VOCABULARY

Correct the sentences.

1 Paul is angry because he losed his smartphone.
Paul is angry because he lost his smartphone.
2 He telled me his name was Sergio.
3 They maked me a delicious chocolate cake.
4 Daisy give me a ticket for the concert yesterday!
5 Last month, we winned a trip to Buenos Aires!
6 I red the paper and then I did the crossword.

3 WORDPOWER *go*

a Complete the conversation with the words in the box.

for   home   ~~out~~   shopping   to   by

MAGGIE Hi, Tina. How was your weekend?
TINA Oh, hello, Maggie. It was really good, thanks. On Saturday night I went [1] _out_ to a restaurant with Steve.
MAGGIE Really? Where?
TINA We went [2] ______ the new Mexican restaurant downtown. It was really good.
MAGGIE But isn't it far from your apartment?
TINA Yes, it is, so we went there [3] ______ bus. And we went [4] ______ by taxi.
MAGGIE Lucky you! Do you want to go [5] ______ a walk?
TINA No, I'm sorry, I can't. I need to go [6] ______. We don't have anything for dinner.
MAGGIE OK, no problem. Talk to you later.

b 06.08 Listen and check.

REVIEW YOUR PROGRESS

Look again at Review Your Progress on p. 68 of the Student's Book. How well can you do these things now?
3 = very well   2 = well   1 = not so well

I CAN ...	
talk about my family and my family history	☐
talk about past activities and hobbies	☐
leave a voicemail message and ask for someone on the phone	☐
write a life story.	☐

7A THE BUS DIDN'T ARRIVE

1 GRAMMAR Simple past: negative and questions

a Complete the sentences with the verbs in the box.

didn't take didn't visit wasn't didn't have
didn't go didn't check ~~didn't stay~~ didn't like

1 They *didn't stay* in the five-star hotel because it was too expensive.
2 She ________ to the Plaza Grande when she was in Quito.
3 I ________ the bus to work this morning. I decided to walk.
4 We ________ the beach because it wasn't very clean.
5 He ________ his uncle when he went to Miami because he was too busy.
6 The weather ________ very nice when we were in London.
7 She ________ enough money to pay for her ticket.
8 They ________ our passports at Glasgow Airport.

b Complete each question with the past simple form of the verb in parentheses.

1 Where *did you go* on vacation last year? (you, go)
2 How ________ from Phoenix to Mexico City? (they, travel)
3 How long ________ from the airport? (be, the drive)
4 How much ________? (the flight, cost)
5 What ________ most about London? (she, like)
6 What ________ of the food in Brazil? (you, think)
7 How long ________ in Boston? (he, stay)
8 How much ________ during your vacation? (you, spend)

2 VOCABULARY Transportation

a Complete the crossword puzzle.

→ Across

2 A ride on a s*peedboat* is a fun way to move across the water quickly.
5 If the weather is good, I ride my b________ to work.
7 He's not old enough to drive a car yet, but he has a s________.
8 In the 19th century, immigrants traveled from Europe to the U.S. by s________.
9 It takes about two hours to travel by t________ from Philadelphia to Washington, D.C.

↓ Down

1 In New York you can take the f________ to visit the Statue of Liberty.
3 When there is a serious accident on the highway, the doctors sometimes arrive by h________.
4 It takes 12 hours by p________ to get to Tokyo from Chicago.
6 There's a special b________ service from downtown to the stadium when there is a soccer game.

3 PRONUNCIATION Sound and spelling: /ɔ/ and /aʊ/

a 07.01 Listen to the words and complete the chart with the words in the box.

~~thought~~ ~~south~~ how ball now
law gone bought mouth house

/ɔ/ (e.g., c**augh**t)	/aʊ/ (e.g., m**ou**se)
thought	*south*

7B I LIKE THE STATIONS

1 GRAMMAR *love / like / don't mind / hate* + verb + *-ing*

a Underline the correct words to complete the sentences.

1 I don't like *studing* / *studying* on the weekend.
2 She loves *traveleing* / *traveling* by train when she visits other countries.
3 My aunt and uncle don't like *driving* / *driveing* in the city.
4 He hates *siting* / *sitting* in traffic in the rush hour.
5 We like *staing* / *staying* in five-star hotels when we go on vacation.
6 I don't mind *taking* / *takeing* the bus if I'm not in a hurry.

b Complete the sentences with the correct forms of the verbs in the box.

not like / take   love / travel   not mind / stay (x2)
love / visit   like / do   ~~hate / study~~   like / watch

1 Mark ___hates___ ___studying___ for school exams.
2 I ________ ________ by train.
3 What ________ you ________ ________ when you're on vacation?
4 Sarah and Jane ________ ________ ________ the subway when it's crowded.
5 She ________ ________ ________ in cheap hotels.
6 We ________ ________ travel documentaries on TV.
7 I ________ ________ ________ in hotels, but I prefer camping.
8 Why ________ you ________ ________ other countries?

2 VOCABULARY Transportation adjectives

a Complete the sentences with the words in the box.

safe   cheap   dirty   empty   comfortable
slow   ~~crowded~~   expensive

1 The subway was really ___crowded___, so we couldn't sit down.
2 We didn't stay at the four-star hotel because it was too ________.
3 Air travel is very ________ these days. There are very few accidents.
4 Don't stay in that hotel – the rooms are very ________. It's horrible.
5 The seats on the plane were very ________, so I went to sleep easily.
6 There were only ten people on the plane. It was almost ________.
7 The bus is very ________. It takes ten hours to get to San Francisco from here.
8 The restaurant was really ________. Our meal only cost six dollars!

b Underline the correct words to complete the sentences.

1 I couldn't sleep on the bus because the seats were really *comfortable* / *crowded* / *uncomfortable*.
2 The train from London to Paris is very *slow* / *fast* / *dirty*. It only takes two and a half hours.
3 I hate traveling on the subway in the summer when it's very *crowded* / *empty* / *cheap*.
4 It's not *clean* / *slow* / *dangerous* to travel alone in this country. People are friendly and always help travelers.
5 Yes, I can recommend that hotel. It's really *clean* / *crowded* / *uncomfortable*.
6 I think six dollars for a subway ticket is very *fast* / *safe* / *expensive*!
7 That taxi was so *empty* / *cheap* / *slow*. It only cost five dollars from the airport!
8 Sorry I'm late. The bus was *empty* / *dirty* / *full*, and I waited 20 minutes for the next one.

3 PRONUNCIATION Word stress

a 07.02 Listen to the words and underline the stressed syllables.

1 comfortable
2 dangerous
3 uncomfortable
4 expensive

7C EVERYDAY ENGLISH
Excuse me, please

1 USEFUL LANGUAGE
Saying *excuse me* and *I'm sorry*

a Complete the mini-conversations with the phrases in the box. (Sometimes there is more than one possible answer.)

It doesn't matter	Excuse me	I'm really sorry
That's OK	I'm so sorry	No problem	~~Excuse me, but~~

A 1 Excuse me, but I think that's my suitcase.
B Is it? 2 ________. I took the wrong one.
A 3 ________. They look the same.

A 4 ________ I didn't come to your party.
B 5 ________. Are you OK?
A I'm all right now, but I didn't feel well yesterday.

A 6 ________. Can you explain that again?
B 7 ________. German grammar is very hard.

b 07.03 Listen and check.

c Match sentences 1–5 with sentences a-e.

1 [e] I'm very sorry I'm late.
2 [ ] I'm sorry I lost your keys.
3 [ ] I'm so sorry I broke your phone.
4 [ ] I'm sorry I hit your car.
5 [ ] I'm really sorry I didn't reply to your message.

a The road was very wet.
b I dropped it on the ground.
c I always lose things.
d Work was very busy today.
e I didn't hear my alarm.

d 07.04 Listen and check.

2 PRONUNCIATION
Emphasizing what we say

a 07.05 Listen to the sentences and underline the stressed words.

1 He's very tired today.
2 I'm so sorry I'm late.
3 We're really busy right now.
4 It's very cold outside.
5 I'm really sorry I can't come.
6 We're so lost!

7D SKILLS FOR WRITING

It really is hard to choose

1 READING

a Adriana Santos, a Brazilian student, studies at a university in Houston. Read her post on *Study Abroad Blog*, a blog about students' lives in other countries. Then check (✓) the correct answer.

The blog talks about:

1 ☐ American transportation, work, and shopping
2 ☐ food, Houston, and studying English
3 ☐ Adriana's family, traveling in Mexico, and her classes
4 ☐ Adriana's homestay family, her classes, and her future plans

b Read Adriana's post on *StudyAbroadBlog* again. Are the sentences true or false?

1 Adriana doesn't like Houston.
2 Adriana likes living with the Henderson family.
3 Adriana has a long walk from the Hendersons' house to the university.
4 Adriana wants to study something new when she goes back to Brazil.
5 Adriana and Antonia want to go on a tour at Space Center Houston.

Study Abroad Blog

The city: Houston's a great city, and it's really big. There are a lot of interesting places to visit, and there are many restaurants and museums, so I'm never bored!

Where I live: I have a room with an American family here. They're very nice. Mr. Henderson's a chef, and Mrs. Henderson's a nurse. They have two children, Zoe and Mark. Zoe loves playing the piano, and Mark likes playing baseball. Their house is near the university, so it only takes about 10 minutes to walk to my classes.

What I do here: My classes are very interesting. My favorite class is North American History. After we finish class, the teacher often goes to a café with us to talk more about our studies. It's a lot of fun! I want to study more history when I go back to Brazil next year.

Who I know: I have a lot of friends in my classes. They're all really friendly. My best friend is Antonia. She's from Guadalajara in Mexico. She's 22, and she loves visiting places in the city with me. We'd like to go on a Level 9 Tour at Space Center Houston, but the tickets are really expensive.

2 WRITING SKILLS Linking ideas with *after*, *when*, and *while*

a Match 1–6 with a–f to make sentences.

1 [e] I'd like to watch a movie
2 ☐ I read my book
3 ☐ When we got to the hotel,
4 ☐ While I'm in Arizona,
5 ☐ I'd like to go to Spain on vacation
6 ☐ She said goodbye to her homestay family

a when they got to the airport.
b after I graduate from college.
c I'd like to visit the Grand Canyon.
d while I was on the beach.
e after I finish my homework.
f we had a quick snack and then went to bed.

3 WRITING

a Imagine you live and study in another country. Write a post on *StudyAbroadBlog*. Try to use linking words (*after*, *when*, *while*). Think about:

- the places in the city
- where you live and who you live with
- your studies
- people you know.

Study Abroad Blog

The city:

____

Where I live:

____

What I do here:

____

Who I know:

____

UNIT 7
Reading and listening extension

1 READING

a Read the text. Are the sentences true or false?

1 Tom loved going to the mountains.
2 He didn't go to the mountains very often.
3 This time, he didn't know how to get home.

b Complete the sentences about the text with the words in the box.

~~cost~~	find	heard	slept	thought	used	walked	went

1 Tom's apartment ___cost___ a lot of money.
2 On the weekend, he ____________ to the mountains.
3 When he walked in the mountains, he ____________ in a tent.
4 He ____________ a lot about his job in the city.
5 On the second day, he tried to ____________ a road.
6 For three days, he ____________ in a straight line.
7 He knew the helicopter was there because he ____________ it.
8 He ____________ his shirt to help the pilot see him.

c Write a short story about a trip with a problem. Think about these questions:

- Why was the person on the trip?
- What was the problem?
- What happened in the end?

LOST IN THE MOUNTAINS!

1 Tom Roberts hated living in the city. He thought it was noisy and crowded, and his apartment was so expensive, he spent most of his money on it.

2 All week at work he thought about the weekends, when he could get away to the country. On Fridays, he packed his tent and some food and water, and caught a bus to the mountains. That was where he felt really happy. He didn't mind camping, even in winter – he just took a very warm sleeping bag!

3 One weekend, he went to the mountains as usual. He followed a path into a forest. He enjoyed the silence and the clean, fresh air. He thought about his job and the city where he lived. He decided that he wanted a new job, away from the city. But what job could he do in the country? He thought about all of this, and he didn't think about where he was going.

4 Then he stopped. He felt cold. It was dark. And he had no idea where he was.

5 He tried to walk in a straight line. He was sure he must come to a road soon! Three days later, he was still walking. By now, he was hungry, dirty and afraid. He started to think that he could never get out of the mountains. Then he heard a strange noise. The noise got louder and louder until at last he saw a helicopter in the air above him.

6 Tom knew this was his last chance. He took off his red shirt, climbed onto a large rock, and waved it. When the helicopter flew closer, he knew he was safe at last.

2 LISTENING

a 07.06 Listen to the conversation. Underline the correct words to complete the sentences.

1 Gloria <u>*has*</u> / *doesn't have* lots of money.
2 Ignacio *has* / *doesn't have* lots of money.
3 Gloria probably *likes* / *doesn't like* vacations like Ignacio's vacation.

b 07.06 Listen to the conversation again. Check (✓) the correct words to complete the sentences.

1 Gloria traveled to California by …
   a ☐ ship.
   b ☑ airplane.
   c ☐ train.
2 Ignacio traveled to California by …
   a ☐ ferry.
   b ☐ bike.
   c ☐ train.
3 While he was in California, Ignacio traveled around by …
   a ☐ train.
   b ☐ ferry.
   c ☐ bike.
4 Ignacio loves riding his bike in …
   a ☐ the city.
   b ☐ towns.
   c ☐ the countryside.
5 Gloria stayed …
   a ☐ in people's homes.
   b ☐ in a hotel.
   c ☐ with friends.
6 Ignacio stayed …
   a ☐ in people's homes.
   b ☐ in a hotel.
   c ☐ with friends.
7 Gloria ate her meals …
   a ☐ in restaurants.
   b ☐ on the beach.
   c ☐ in cafés.
8 At the end of her vacation, Gloria …
   a ☐ took her plane.
   b ☐ caught her plane.
   c ☐ missed her plane.

c Write a conversation between two people about vacations. One has a lot of money, and one doesn't.

- Describe where each person went and the things they did.
- What difference did it make to have a lot of money or not much money?

Review and extension

1 GRAMMAR

Correct the sentences.

1 Did you watched the soccer game last night?
   Did you watch the soccer game last night?
2 We didn't stayed in expensive hotels.
3 I didn't liked the food in that restaurant.
4 **A** Did they catch the last bus?
   B Yes, they do.
5 He didn't came to the movie theater with us because he was tired.
6 Did you bought your sunglasses in the supermarket?
7 Nick didn't wanted to wait for the bus.
8 **A** Did he go to his grandparents' house on Sunday?
   B No, he don't.

2 VOCABULARY

Correct the sentences.

1 Jack lost his plane and waited five hours for the next one.
   Jack missed his plane and waited five hours for the next one.
2 We hit the train every day at 8 o'clock.
3 Get up at the next stop for the museum.
4 You don't check planes to go to Sydney. It's a direct flight.
5 I didn't put on the bus because it was full.
6 Mary gives the subway to go downtown.

3 WORDPOWER *get*

Change one verb in each sentence to the correct form of the verb *get*.

1 Are you thirsty? Have a glass of water.
   Are you thirsty? Get a glass of water.
2 He becomes angry when we're late for class.
3 We arrived here early today.
4 I received a letter from an old friend last week.
5 I bought a new bag this morning.

REVIEW YOUR PROGRESS

Look again at Review Your Progress on p. 78 of the Student's Book. How well can you do these things now?
3 = very well   2 = well   1 = not so well

I CAN …	
talk about past travels	☐
talk about what I like and dislike about transportation	☐
say *excuse me* and *I'm sorry*	☐
write an email about myself.	☐

8A THEY CAN DO THINGS MOST PEOPLE CAN'T

1 GRAMMAR *can / can't*; *could / couldn't* for ability

a Look at the questionnaire about Adrian and complete the sentences with *can* or *can't*.

1 Adrian ___can___ ski pretty well, but he ___can't___ skate at all.
2 **TOM** ______ you ride a horse, Adrian?
ADRIAN No, I ______, but I ______ ride a bike really well!
3 Adrian ______ sing very well. He ______ play the piano pretty well, but he ______ play the guitar at all.
4 **TOM** ______ you do yoga?
ADRIAN Yes, I ______ do yoga really well.
5 He ______ do karate pretty well, but he ______ do judo at all.

Adrian's abilities questionnaire

	Yes, really well	Yes, pretty well	No, not very well	No, not at all
ski?		✓		
skate?				✓
ride a horse?				✓
ride a bike?	✓			
sing?			✓	
play the piano?		✓		
play the guitar?				✓
do yoga?	✓			
do judo?				✓
do karate?		✓		

b Underline the correct words to complete the sentences.

1 My mother *can / couldn't / can't* swim when she was a child, but now she *can / could / couldn't* swim five kilometers.
2 **A** *Can / Can't / Could* you play tennis when you were five?
B No, I *can't / couldn't / could.*
3 **A** *Can / Can't / Couldn't* you speak Spanish?
B No, not now. I *can / can't / could* speak it when I lived in Mexico, but not any more.
4 When I started biking, I *can't / couldn't / can* ride very far, but now I *could / can / can't* ride ten kilometers without stopping.
5 He *could / can't / can* dance all night when he was a young man, but not these days.
6 I usually work on the weekends, so I *could / can / can't* play golf very often.

2 VOCABULARY Sports and exercise

a Complete the sentences.

1 He went ___running___ every day after work because he wanted to get in shape for the Boston Marathon.
2 My son plays American ______ for his high school. He wears big shoulder pads and a helmet.
3 John loves going ______. He likes spending the day by the river. When he catches something, he likes to cook it for dinner.
4 I went to Switzerland last winter, and I went ______ in the mountains every day.
5 Sometimes I do ______ in the evening. It helps me to relax before I go to bed.
6 Alice loves going ______ at the community pool. The water is always nice and warm.
7 I like playing ______ on the beach. You only need four people, a ball, and a net.
8 In Argentina, I learned to ______ the tango.
9 In Quebec, it's so cold in the winter that you can ______ on the river.
10 Last summer, we went ______ on a big boat on the Mediterranean Sea for a week. I'd love to do it again.

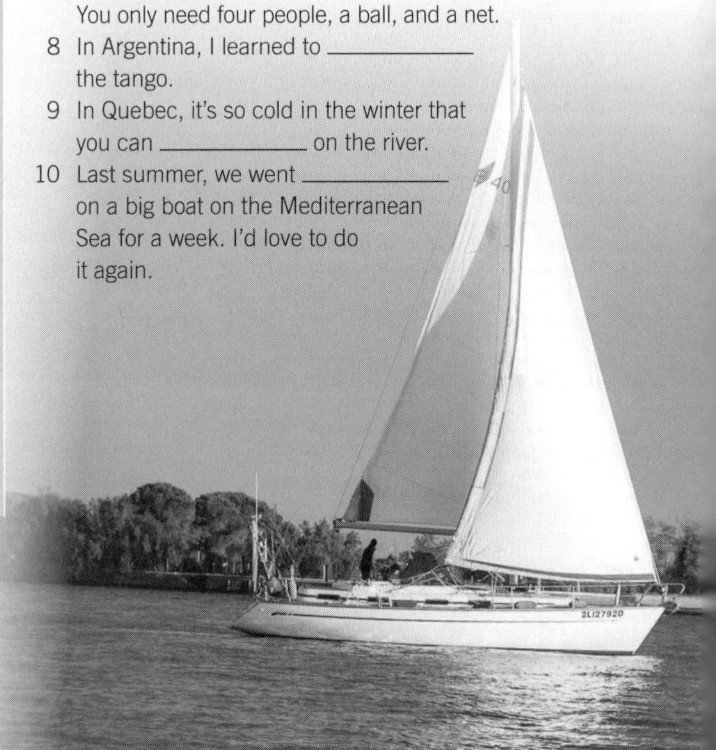

8B HOW EASY IS IT TO GET IN SHAPE?

1 GRAMMAR *have to / don't have to*

a Underline the correct words to complete the sentences.

1 **A** *You have to / Do you have to / Have you to* really be in shape to run a half marathon?
B Yes, *you have / you have to / you do*. You *have to / have / has to* train hard for several months.

2 They learned Spanish when they lived in Spain, so they *haven't to / don't have to / doesn't have to* study hard for the Spanish exam.

3 If you want to become a really good athlete, you *have to / has to / haven't to* train every day.

4 **A** *Had you to / You had to / Did you have to* take a taxi to the airport?
B Yes, *we did / we had to / we had.*

5 **A** *Have you to / Do you have to / You have to* go to the gym every day if you want to get in shape?
B No, *you haven't / you have not / you don't*, but you *has to / have to / have* go three times a week.

b Complete each sentence with the correct form of *have to*.

1 **A** ___Do___ you ___have to___ bring your own skis?
B No, you __________. You can rent them for the day.

2 You __________ pay to use the gym for a day. It's free if you want to try it.

3 Sometimes she can work from home, so she __________ go to the office every day.

4 In some countries, children __________ go to school in the evenings. I think it's better to go in the mornings.

5 **A** __________ I __________ become a member to use the swimming pool?
B Yes, you __________.

6 **A** What time __________ she __________ catch the bus to school in the morning?
B She __________ take the bus at 7:30 because she lives far from her school.

2 VOCABULARY Parts of the body

a Match the parts of the body in the picture with the words in the box.

arm hand leg foot stomach head neck knee

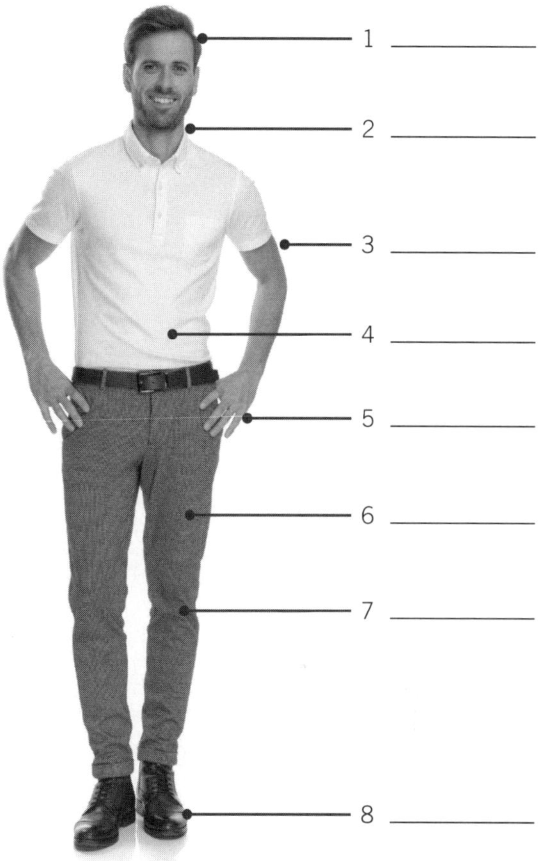

b Complete the crossword puzzle.

→ Across

4 He can't hold a pen or pencil because he broke two of his ___fingers___ in the accident.

6 I don't like dancing with you. You always step on my __________. They really hurt after!

7 This bed is really uncomfortable. It hurts my __________.

↓ Down

1 I think these shoes are too small for me. They hurt my __________.

2 You have a thumb and four fingers on each __________.

3 You have to have strong __________ to run a marathon.

4 He can't walk very far because his __________ hurts. He broke it last week on a ski trip.

5 When I sleep on a plane, my head falls to the side, and then my __________ hurts.

8 Lucas broke his __________ when he went skiing last weekend.

8C EVERYDAY ENGLISH
I'm a little tired

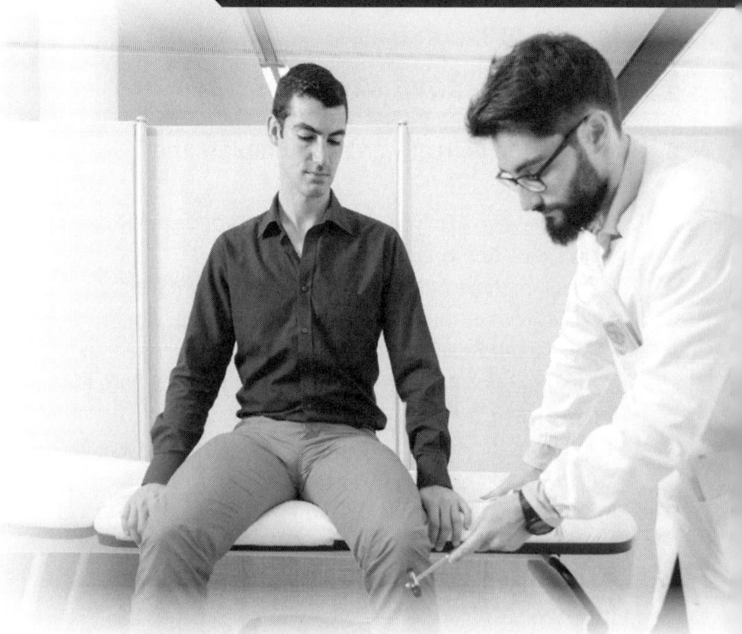

1 USEFUL LANGUAGE Talking about health and how you feel

a Match questions 1–5 with answers a–e.

1 [c] What's the matter?
2 [ ] How do you feel?
3 [ ] Are you all right?
4 [ ] Does your knee hurt?
5 [ ] Do you have a fever?

a Yes, it does. It hurts when I walk.
b No, I don't. I just feel a little tired.
c Nothing. I've just have a stomachache.
d Yes, I'm fine now, thanks.
e Well, actually, I feel terrible.

b 08.01 Listen and check.

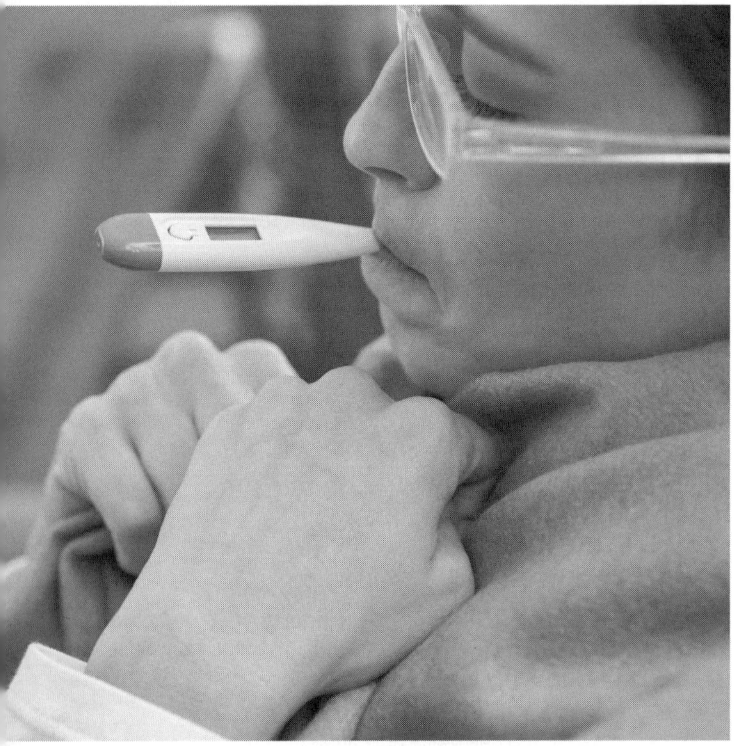

c Put the conversation in the correct order.

[ ] **TONY** Do you have a fever?
[ ] **JUDY** I'm not sure. I don't feel very well.
[ ] **JUDY** OK, thanks.
[1] **TONY** Hi, Judy. Good to see you. How are you?
[ ] **TONY** Oh, no! Why don't you go home and go to bed? I can finish your work today.
[ ] **JUDY** Hi, Tony. Not so great today.
[ ] **JUDY** Yes, maybe, and I have a terrible headache.
[ ] **TONY** Oh, I'm sorry to hear that. What's the matter?

d 08.02 Listen and check.

2 PRONUNCIATION Connecting words

a 08.03 Listen to the sentences. Check (✓) the two words that are connected together.

1 That man over there doesn't dance very well.
a [ ] very well b [✓] doesn't dance
2 I'm sorry, but I can't talk right now.
a [ ] I'm sorry b [ ] can't talk
3 Thank you very much, ma'am. Have a good day.
a [ ] very much b [ ] good day
4 We have a really big garden at our house.
a [ ] big garden b [ ] our house
5 There's a small lake in the middle of the park.
a [ ] small lake b [ ] the park

8D SKILLS FOR WRITING
However, I improved quickly

1 READING

a Every month, *Pastimes* magazine interviews a reader about their hobby. Read Nick Delgado's interview and check (✓) the best answer.

Nick likes taking photos …
1 ☐ when he goes on vacation with friends.
2 ☐ of different people and places.
3 ☐ when there is a competition he can enter.

b Read the interview again. Are the sentences true or false?

1 ☐ Nick became interested in photography when he saw his friend's photos of Machu Picchu.
2 ☐ Nick's first camera wasn't very expensive.
3 ☐ Nick prefers to print his photos to show people.
4 ☐ Nick's grandfather won a prize in the photography competition.
5 ☐ Nick wants to become a professional photographer.

Nick, tell us why you started your hobby.

Two years ago, a friend showed me some photos from his vacation in Peru. His photos of Machu Picchu were really amazing, so I decided to start taking photos, too.

So, what did you do next?

I bought a cheap camera and carried it everywhere with me. I took photos of my family, my friends, and the countryside near my town.
I joined a photography club and slowly improved. However, I only had an old laptop, and I couldn't see the photos very well or show them to friends easily. I decided to buy a computer with a really big screen. Now everyone can see the photos clearly, and I can make changes to the colors quickly and easily.

Last month, I entered a photography competition, and a photo of my grandfather won first prize. I was so happy! I won $500, so I bought a fantastic new camera.

What would you like to do with your hobby in the future?

I'd really like to be a professional photographer. However, there aren't a lot of jobs for photographers, so right now it's only a hobby.

2 WRITING SKILLS
Adverbs of manner

a Complete the sentences with adverbs formed from the adjectives in parentheses.

1 The Tour de France riders cycled ___slowly___ (slow) up the mountain and then went down the other side really ___fast___ (fast).
2 My soccer team lost the game 8–0 because we played very ____________ (bad).
3 If you listen ____________ (careful), you can hear the sound of the ocean in the distance.
4 When you travel, you can make new friends ____________ (easy).
5 My phone doesn't work very ____________ (good) here, so please speak ____________ (clear).
6 You can fly to New York very ____________ (cheap) these days.

3 WRITING

a Think about the hobby/sport of a family member or a famous person you like. Write answers to the questions. Remember to use adverbs.

When and why did he/she start the hobby/sport?

____
____
____
____
____

What did he/she do (e.g., clubs, competitions)?

____
____
____
____
____

What would he/she like to do with the hobby/sport in the future?

____
____
____
____
____

UNIT 8
Reading and listening extension

1 READING

a Read the magazine article. Check (✓) the best description of what it says.

1 ☐ Triathlons are very difficult, and you can only do them if you are in very good shape.

2 ☐ There are triathlons at different levels, so you can find one that is right for you. You can prepare for a triathlon at any level.

3 ☐ It is easy to swim, bike, or run, but it is difficult to do all three with no rest in between. It is best not to try to do these things together.

b Read the magazine article again and complete the sentences.

1 In the first part of the triathlon you have to ___swim___, often in a lake or the ocean.

2 When you swim in the ocean, you can't usually put your __________ down.

3 When you practice swimming, lift your __________ a long way out of the water.

4 In the second part of the triathlon, you have to __________ a bike.

5 It's dangerous to get too __________ to the other bikes.

6 When you start to run, you usually feel __________.

c Write an email to a friend who never does any sports. Give him or her some ideas about one or two sports to try and some advice on how to prepare. Include at least one sentence with *have to* and one with *don't have to*.

HOW TO PREPARE FOR A TRIATHLON

So, you can swim, you can ride a bike, and you go running twice a week. But all three things together... Are you crazy?

Many people like the idea of a triathlon, but they're worried that it's too difficult for them. If that's you, remember, you don't have to start with the Olympics. There are a lot of triathlons for beginners.

So read our advice and start preparing for your first triathlon. *You can do it*!

SWIMMING

For many people, it's the first part, swimming, that they're most worried about. It's often in a lake or the ocean, so even if you get tired, you can't put your feet down for a rest. Also, you have to lift your arms up high because the water moves up and down. It's a good idea to practice this, even when you're in the swimming pool.

CYCLING

This is the second part of the triathlon. Riding a bike with a lot of other people can be strange at first, so practice with friends. Remember that in the race, you have to stay away from the other bikes because it's dangerous to get too close.

RUNNING

The running part is often very hard because you have to do it when you're already tired. When you get off the bike, you may think you can't even stand up! So make sure you practice riding your bike and then running at least once a week.

GOOD LUCK!

2 LISTENING

a 08.04 Listen to the conversation. Are the sentences true or false?

1 Rosa can play badminton today.
2 Rosa and Emilia talk about doing exercises for Rosa's back.
3 Rosa and Emilia don't want to try yoga.

b 08.04 Listen to the conversation again. Who are the sentences about, Rosa (R) or Emilia (E)?

1 [R] Her back hurts.
2 [ ] Her dad has problems with his back.
3 [ ] Her mom does yoga.
4 [ ] She can't touch her toes.
5 [ ] She fell down when she was ice skating.
6 [ ] She has a class at two.
7 [ ] She has to be careful about her back.
8 [ ] She is learning to play the piano.
9 [ ] She needs to find another friend to play badminton.
10 [ ] She says there are yoga classes online.
11 [ ] She thinks yoga is difficult.

c 08.04 Listen again. Underline the correct words to complete the sentences.

1 Rosa fell and hurt her *leg* / *back* / *hand*.
2 She was skating with her *friend* / *mom* / *sister*.
3 When she fell, it *didn't hurt much* / *hurt a lot* / *hurt a little*.
4 Rosa's *sister* / *dad* / *mom* has a bad back too.
5 Emilia's mom says that *yoga* / *badminton* / *skating* is good for your back.
6 Rosa and Emilia decide to *go to a yoga class* / *play badminton* / *go ice skating*.

d Write about the sports you play. Think about these questions:

- Which sports do you play?
- What do you have to do?
- Why do you like the sports?

If you don't play any sports, write about why not. Think about these questions:

- Why don't you play any sports?
- Is there a reason you can't play them?
- Which sports would you like to try and why?

Review and extension

1 GRAMMAR

Correct the sentences.

1 My brother can skiing very well.
My brother can ski very well.
2 When I was 15, I could ran 100 meters in 12 seconds.
3 I'm sorry I couldn't coming to your party.
4 My grandfather can't to see very well without his glasses.
5 Can you dancing the tango?
6 He couldn't to play soccer after he broke his leg.
7 Helen could drove when she was 17.
8 Could you to ride a bike when you were five?

2 VOCABULARY

Correct the sentences.

1 When they were at the beach, they played soccer and voleyball.
When they were at the beach, they played soccer and volleyball.
2 We went runing after work yesterday.
3 I love skying in the winter.
4 We don't play tenis in the rain.
5 Snowbording is a very popular sport in Chile.
6 I don't like going fisching. It's so boring!
7 I couldn't danse very well before I took lessons.
8 He goes swiming every day before work.

3 WORDPOWER *tell / say*

Complete the sentences with the words in the box.

told say tells ~~said~~ tell said

1 Clare ___said___ sorry for being late.
2 I ________ my wife I was at the airport.
3 Please ________ sorry to your sister that I forgot her birthday.
4 My uncle always ________ us about what he did in the war.
5 We ________ goodbye at the airport last night.
6 Can you ________ me how to get to the train station please?

REVIEW YOUR PROGRESS

Look again at Review Your Progress on p. 88 of the Student's Book. How well can you do these things now?
3 = very well 2 = well 1 = not so well

I CAN ...	
talk about past and present abilities	[ ]
talk about sports and exercise	[ ]
talk about the body and getting in shape	[ ]
talk about health and how I feel	[ ]
write an article.	[ ]

9A WE'RE NOT BUYING ANYTHING

1 VOCABULARY Shopping

a Write the names of the places in a shopping mall under the pictures.

1 department store

2 ______

3 ______

4 ______

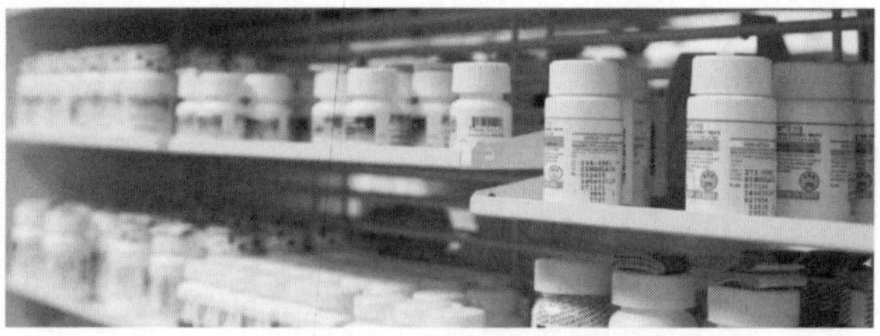

5 ______

6 ______

2 GRAMMAR Present continuous

a Underline the correct words to complete the sentences.

1 **A** What *do you doing* / *are you doing* / *you are doing* here?
B I *'m waiting* / *'s waiting* / *waiting* for my brother.
2 **A** Where *Michael is going* / *Michael going* / *'s Michael going*?
B *He looking* / *He's looking* / *Is he looking* for his brother.
3 **A** *Are you having* / *You're having* / *You having* dinner now?
B Yes, *we do* / *we're having* / *we are*. We *having* / *are have* / *'re having* empanadas.
4 **A** What *you're buying* / *are you buying* / *you buying*?
B I *'m not buying* / *not buying* / *'m not buy* anything. I *just looking* / *just are looking* / *'m just looking*.
5 **A** It *'s raining not* / *not raining* / *'s not raining* right now.
B In fact, the sun *shining* / *are shining* / *'s shining*.

b 09.01 Listen and check.

c Complete the sentences with the present continuous form of the verbs in parentheses. Use contractions where possible.

1 **A** What _'s Silvia doing_? (Silvia, do)
B She ______ (get) ready to go out.
2 **A** Who ______ (you, wait) for?
B I ______ (wait) for my friend.
3 **A** ______ (you and Maria, have) a good time in Miami?
B No, ______ (not). We ______ (stay) at a terrible hotel.
4 **A** What ______ (you, read) right now?
B I ______ (read) the new novel by the author of the Harry Potter books.
5 Julian ______ (buy) some new jeans.
6 How funny! Rodrigo and Martin ______ (wear) the same shirt!

3 PRONUNCIATION Word stress in compound nouns

a 09.02 Listen and decide which word is stressed. Check (✓) the stressed word.

1 This is one of the biggest shopping malls in the world.
a ☑ shopping b ☐ mall
2 There are over two hundred and fifty clothing stores.
a ☐ clothing b ☐ stores
3 There are about twenty-three bookstores.
a ☐ book b ☐ stores
4 If you can't find a store, you can ask someone at the information desk for help.
a ☐ information b ☐ desk
5 It can be hard to find a space in the parking lot.
a ☐ parking b ☐ lot
6 A lot of people prefer to wait for a bus at the bus stop.
a ☐ bus b ☐ stop

9B EVERYONE'S DANCING IN THE STREETS

1 GRAMMAR Simple present or present continuous

a Underline the correct words to complete the conversation.

KARLA Hi, Julian. What [1] *do you buy* / *are you buying*?
JULIAN Hello, Karla. [2] *I'm buying* / *I buy* some new pants.
KARLA But [3] *you're usually wearing* / *you usually wear* jeans and sneakers.
JULIAN Yes, [4] *I'm knowing* / *I know*. [5] *I'm trying* / *I try* to dress well for my new job.
KARLA Well, [6] *I'm liking* / *I like* them.
JULIAN Good, and, look, [7] *I wear* / *I'm wearing* some new shoes that I bought yesterday.
KARLA Wow, [8] *they're looking* / *they look* great!
JULIAN Thanks. [9] *Are you wearing* / *Do you wear* a new dress?
KARLA Yes, [10] *I do* / *I am*. What [11] *are you thinking* / *do you think*?
JULIAN It's really nice. Hey, [12] *do you want* / *are you wanting* to get some coffee?
KARLA Sorry, I can't. [13] *I wait* / *I'm waiting* for my brother. [14] *He's parking* / *He parks* the car.
JULIAN OK, no problem. Bye!

b 09.03 Listen and check.

c Complete the sentences. Use the simple present or present continuous forms of the verbs in the box.

walk spend cost drink ~~wear~~
watch wait go rain ~~like~~

1 Karen never ___wears___ dresses to work. She ___likes___ wearing pants.
2 He can't talk to you right now. He __________ a soccer game on TV.
3 I __________ for you in front of the train station. Don't be late!
4 We normally __________ orange juice with breakfast and water with lunch.
5 It __________ more than $1,000 to buy a ticket for the World Cup!
6 It __________ hard now, so we can't go for a walk by the river.
7 We often __________ our vacation days in the mountains.
8 Yes, we usually __________ home by bus, but we __________ home now.

2 VOCABULARY Clothes

a Complete the crossword puzzle.

→ Across
2 I usually wear blue __________. But I have other kinds of pants, too.
4 You wear __________ to cover your feet. They are very soft.
7 My grandma gave me this beautiful __________. Unfortunately, it's too small for my finger.
8 Look at those dark clouds! Why don't you take your __________ with you?
11 It's more comfortable to wear __________ on a hot day than pants.

↓ Down
1 That wedding ___dress___ costs $13,000. It's too expensive!
3 At my sister's school, the boys have to wear pants, and the girls have to wear a __________.
5 David needs a new white __________ and a tie to wear for his job interview on Monday.
6 Your hands look so cold! Where are your __________?
9 If you want to know the time, look at your __________.
10 In the snow, you should wear __________ on your feet. They keep your feet warm and dry.

3 PRONUNCIATION Sounds and spelling: *o*

a 09.04 Listen to the words with *o*. Complete the chart with the words in the box.

~~vote~~ some soup dollar rock pool other toe
boat brother cool on watch do love hope

/ɑ/ (e.g., *sock*)	/u/ (e.g., *boot*)	/ʌ/ (e.g., *glove*)	/oʊ/ (e.g., *coat*)
			vote

9C EVERYDAY ENGLISH
It looks really good on you

1 USEFUL LANGUAGE
Choosing and paying for clothes

a Match questions 1–6 with answers a–f.

1 [d] Can I help you?
2 [ ] Can I try them on?
3 [ ] What size are you?
4 [ ] What color would you like?
5 [ ] What do you think?
6 [ ] How much are these jeans?

a Blue or green, please.
b 32, I think.
c They're $49.99.
d Yes, I'm looking for a red dress and some black shoes.
e It looks really good on you.
f Sure. The fitting rooms are over there.

b 09.05 Listen and check.

c Put the words in the correct order to make sentences.

1 looking / some / for / jeans / I'm .
I'm looking for some jeans.
2 a / I'm / 10 / size .
______
3 would / color / like / what / you ?
______
4 size / think / I / are / these / your .
______
5 over / fitting / rooms / the / there / right / are .
______
6 you / on / they / great / look .
______
7 them / take / I'll .
______
8 I / card / by / credit / pay / can ?
______

2 PRONUNCIATION Connecting words

a 09.06 Listen to the sentences. Check (✓) the two words that are connected together.

1 I'm a size 10.
a [✓] I'm a
b [ ] size 10
2 It looks good on you.
a [ ] good on
b [ ] on you
3 How much is it?
a [ ] How much
b [ ] much is
4 The jeans are over there.
a [ ] The jeans
b [ ] jeans are

9D SKILLS FOR WRITING
Thank you for the nice present

1 READING

a Read the four thank-you emails. Which email is from … ?

a ☐ someone who was sick recently
b ☐ someone who had a problem with her car
c ☐ a family member
d [1] someone who left her company

1

Inbox

Dear Mr. Jones,

I'd just like to thank you very much for the gift card you gave me for a going-away present. I'm excited to start using it right away. Best of luck in the future.

Regards,
Lisa

2

◀ Inbox

Hello Grandma,

Thanks so much for the shirt you gave me for my birthday. It's a wonderful present! Blue's my favorite color, and my friends say it looks really good on me.

Love,
Tina

3

Mail

Hi Paul,

Many thanks for your help when my car didn't start last night. I really need to buy a new one!

Thanks again,
Julie

4

1 of 35

Dear Sarah,

I just want to say thank you for the beautiful flowers you sent me when I was in the hospital last week. I feel much better now, and the flowers look beautiful on my kitchen table.

See you soon,
Hannah

b Read the emails again. Are the sentences true or false?

1 Lisa bought Mr. Jones a gift card when she left her job.
2 Tina didn't like the birthday present from her grandmother.
3 Julie helped Paul start his car yesterday.
4 Hannah isn't in the hospital this week.

2 WRITING SKILLS Writing formal and informal emails

a Add one word to each sentence to make it correct.

1 I just wanted to thank you the wonderful present you gave me.
I just wanted to thank you for the wonderful present you gave me.
2 Thanks much for the book you sent me for my birthday.
______
3 I just wanted thank you for the flowers.
______
4 Thank for the chocolates. They were delicious!
______
5 I just like to say thank you for inviting me to your party on Saturday.
______

3 WRITING

a Write two thank-you emails. Use the information in the boxes and the emails in 1a to help you.

Email 1
To: Sonia
Relationship: your friend
Reason for writing: to thank her for her help when you moved to a new apartment
Extra information: the new apartment = lovely, invite her for dinner soon?
From: Iris

Email 2
To: Ana
Relationship: your mom's neighbor
Reason for writing: to thank her for taking care of your cat (Mittens) when you were on vacation
Extra information: wonderful vacation, cup of coffee at your house?
From: Miguel

UNIT 9
Reading and listening extension

1 READING

a Read the two emails. Complete the sentences.

1 Owen sent Rafael an <u>invitation</u> to visit him.
2 Rafael wants to know about the ____________ where Owen lives.
3 Owen describes the stores and coffee shops in his ____________.
4 Owen tells Rafael about the ____________ in Seattle in the summer.
5 Owen tells Rafael what ____________ he needs to bring.

To: Owen
From: Rafael
Subject: Re: Invitation

Dear Owen,

Thank you very much for your invitation to visit you in the summer. I asked my parents, and they say they can give me the money for the ticket, so that's great!

I'm writing this on my phone in a coffee shop in Italy because we're spending a week here, skiing. It's snowing now, so it seems strange to think about summer! Tell me more about where you live. Is it a big city? Is there a lot to do there?

Also, what is the weather like in the summer? My sister says it's always raining in Seattle, but I think she just wants to make me angry!

Write back soon!

Rafael

b Complete the sentences with the words in the box. There are some extra words.

countryside	difficult	fun	food	~~invited~~
coffee shops	sister	Italy	the U.S.	weather

1 Owen <u>invited</u> Rafael to visit him.
2 Rafael and his family are skiing in ____________.
3 Rafael's ____________ isn't always nice to him.
4 There are a lot of ____________ in Owen's neighborhood.
5 It is ____________ to be in a city where there are many things to do.
6 The ____________ in the summer is usually hot.

c A friend from another country is coming to visit you. Write an email describing the place where you live and the clothes your friend needs to bring.

To: Rafael
From: Owen
Date: February 4 at 10:26
Subject: Re: Invitation

Dear Rafael,

Thanks for your email. I'm so happy that your parents said yes!

So, to answer your questions: I live in a big city. My neighborhood has a big post office, some interesting stores, and a lot of coffee shops where we can meet my friends.

Bring your sneakers because we will be doing a lot of walking, so I can show you the popular tourist places. We can also take the bus to a lot of places. There's so much to do here!

It's usually pretty hot in the summer, so if you want to stay indoors, I can take you to a shopping mall or we can go to the movie theater. But if you want to be outside, we can go to the beach. So bring a swimsuit, some T-shirts, and shorts. It gets a little cooler in the evenings, so you will probably need jeans and a light sweater. It doesn't rain all the time (tell your sister!), but it's still a good idea to bring a raincoat. Also, pack a nice pair of pants and shoes in case we go to a nice restaurant.

Enjoy the rest of your ski trip!
I can't wait to hear all about it.

Talk to you soon,

Owen

2 LISTENING

a 09.07 Listen to the conversation. Are the sentences true or false?

1 The family is having a birthday party for Grandma.
2 Brad and Gloria like what their dad is wearing.
3 Their grandmother will like what their dad is wearing.
4 Their dad has a good reason for wearing the sweater.

b 09.07 Listen to the conversation again and check (✓) the correct answers.

1 What is on Dad's sweater?
a ☐ a sheep
b ☑ an elephant
c ☐ eleven animals

2 What do Mom and Dad get from the kitchen?
a ☐ glasses
b ☐ a different sweater
c ☐ sandwiches

3 What is the special day?
a ☐ Grandma's birthday
b ☐ Shelly's birthday
c ☐ Dad's birthday

4 Why does Grandma arrive early?
a ☐ to see Dad's sweater
b ☐ to eat some food
c ☐ to help make the food

5 What food is Mom making when Grandma arrives?
a ☐ pizza
b ☐ cakes
c ☐ sandwiches

6 Why does Dad say he needs to take off his sweater?
a ☐ he's too hot
b ☐ his children don't like it
c ☐ it's dirty

7 What is Dad wearing under the sweater?
a ☐ an old shirt
b ☐ a T-shirt
c ☐ his best shirt

8 Why did Dad wear the sweater?
a ☐ to please his mom
b ☐ to please his wife
c ☐ to make his children angry

c Think of somewhere special you went, for example a party or for a meal in an expensive restaurant. Write about the clothes that you and other people wore.

Review and extension

1 GRAMMAR

Correct the sentences. (Sometimes there is more than one possible answer.)

1 Hi, Sally! I really enjoy my vacation in Colorado.
Hi, Sally! I'm really enjoying my vacation in Colorado.
2 My friend Mario is speaking English very well.
3 Sorry, it's time to go because my train comes.
4 She's wait for us outside the movie theater.
5 Tony's in that store over there. He buys a newspaper.
6 I'm usually going to the movie theater on the weekends.
7 John's at the library. He's studies for his exams.
8 Are you liking Italian food?

2 VOCABULARY

Correct the sentences.

1 Jane is looking for a new dress in that new clothings' store.
Jane is looking for a new dress in that new clothing store.
2 The parcking lot across the street is open all night.
3 He's waiting for us at the main entrace.
4 The booksstore closes at 5:30.
5 Excuse me. What's the prize of these jeans?
6 Here are your T-shirts. The reciept is in the bag.
7 I like your new skarf. It's very nice.
8 My boyfriend bought me these earings for my birthday.

3 WORDPOWER *time*

Complete the sentences with the words in the box.

took save spend ~~waste~~ spare find nice

1 Don't *waste* time trying to find the street on your GPS. Just ask that woman over there.
2 It ________ him a long time to learn Chinese.
3 She loves going for long walks in her ________ time.
4 We can ________ time if we walk this way.
5 I hope you had a ________ time in Brazil.
6 It's really important to ________ time with your children when they are little.
7 I can never ________ time to read books.

REVIEW YOUR PROGRESS

Look again at Review Your Progress on p. 98 of the Student's Book. How well can you do these things now?
3 = very well 2 = well 1 = not so well

I CAN ...	
say where I am and what I'm doing	☐
talk about the clothes I wear at different times	☐
shop for clothes	☐
write a thank-you email.	☐

10A THEY'RE MORE COMFORTABLE THAN EARBUDS

1 GRAMMAR Comparative adjectives

a Underline the correct words to complete the sentences.

1 My new laptop is *more light than* / *<u>lighter than</u>* / *lighter that* yours.
2 I think headphones are *more useful* / *usefuller* / *useful more* than earbuds.
3 Gary's tablet is *biger* / *more big* / *bigger* than this one.
4 Our camera is *heavier* / *more heavy* / *heavyer* than theirs.
5 In my opinion, tablets are *difficulter* / *more difficult* / *difficult* to use than computers.
6 The camera on my new phone is *gooder* / *more good* / *better* than the camera on my old phone.
7 Texting my friends is *easier* / *more easy* / *easyer* than emailing them.
8 The traffic in New York is *worser* / *worse* / *badder* than the traffic in Chicago.

b Look at the information about the two TVs and complete the sentences. Use the comparative forms of the adjectives in the box.

Television	HiTek TV	PicX TV
1 Weight	18 kilos	16 kilos
2 Screen size	140 centimeters	150 centimeters
3 Picture quality	★★★★☆	★★★★★
4 Sound quality	★★★★☆	★★★☆☆
5 Easy to use?	★★★☆☆	★★★★★
6 Appearance	★★☆☆☆	★★★☆☆
7 First sold	December 2020	February 2022
8 Price	$550	$495

attractive new good easy expensive ~~heavy~~ clear big

1 **Weight:** The HiTek TV is ___heavier___ than the PicX TV.
2 **Screen size:** The PicX TV is ____________ than the HiTek TV.
3 **Picture quality:** The picture on the PicX TV is ____________ than on the HiTek TV.
4 **Sound quality:** The sound is ____________ on the HiTek TV than on the PicX TV.
5 **Easy to use?** The PicX TV is ____________ to use than the HiTek TV.
6 **Appearance:** The PicX TV is ____________ than the HiTek TV.
7 **First sold:** The PicX TV is ____________ than the HiTek TV.
8 **Price:** The HiTek TV is ____________ than the PicX TV.

2 VOCABULARY IT collocations

a Match 1–5 with a–e to make sentences.

1 [c] Click on
2 [ ] Enter your username and password to log in to
3 [ ] Click here to download
4 [ ] He forgot to save
5 [ ] For more information about our products, visit

a our website or call this number.
b the document before closing down his computer.
c this link to watch our new video clip.
d powerful antivirus software. Keep your computer safe.
e the computers in this library.

b Underline the correct words to complete the sentences.

1 No, you can't *download* / *<u>log in to</u>* my computer. It's private!
2 You can use my laptop to *check* / *visit* your email.
3 When you *save* / *visit* their website, they give a dollar to help poor people.
4 You should *check* / *save* your document every 15 minutes.
5 You can listen to her new song if you click on this *link* / *computer*.
6 Please don't download any unsafe *websites* / *files* to my computer.
7 I like to *go* / *click* online and watch videos.

10B WHAT'S THE MOST BEAUTIFUL LANGUAGE IN THE WORLD?

1 GRAMMAR Superlative adjectives

a <u>Underline</u> the correct words to complete the sentences.

1. They say that Arabic is one of *the more difficult* / *<u>the most difficult</u>* / *the difficultest* languages *of the world* / *than the world* / *<u>in the world</u>*.
2. Spanish is one of *the most popular* / *most popular* / *the popularest* languages *for learn* / *to learn* / *for learning*.
3. In 2018, *the goodest* / *the best* / *the most good* female tennis player was Simona Halep.
4. I work in one of *the noisyest* / *the most noisy* / *the noisiest* areas *in the city* / *at the city* / *on the city*.
5. I think Xhosa is *the more strange* / *the strangest* / *the most strange* language! I heard people speaking it in South Africa.
6. I think Brazil is *the interestingest* / *most interesting* / *the most interesting* country to visit *in South America* / *of South America* / *by South America*.
7. The Internet is one of *the more useful* / *the most useful* / *the usefulest* inventions of the 20th century.
8. He's one of *the most famous* / *the famousest* / *the more famous* actors in Hollywood.

b Put the words in the correct order to make sentences.

1. funniest / one / of the / on TV / he's / people .
   He's one of the funniest people on TV.
2. Japanese / languages / is / hardest / to learn / the / one of.
   ____
3. the / Sam / best / in our class / student / is .
   ____
4. was / the / day / wettest / last Tuesday / of the year .
   ____
5. one of / beautiful / the / she's / women / most / in the world .
   ____
6. is / the / which / city / biggest / in the world ?
   ____
7. we / last year / the / had / winter / since 1986 / coldest .
   ____
8. in the world / the / land animal / the cheetah / fastest / is .
   ____

2 VOCABULARY High numbers

a Check (✓) the correct words.

1 7,500
- a ☐ seven hundred and fifty
- b ☑ seven thousand five hundred
- c ☐ seven million five hundred thousand

2 812
- a ☐ eight hundred twelve
- b ☐ eight thousand and twelve
- c ☐ eight hundred and twelve

3 2,500,000
- a ☐ two million five hundred thousand
- b ☐ two thousand five hundred
- c ☐ twenty-five hundred thousand

4 1,299
- a ☐ twelve hundred ninety-nine
- b ☐ one thousand, two hundred and ninety-nine
- c ☐ one million two hundred and ninety-nine thousand

5 2001
- a ☐ two thousand and one
- b ☐ two thousand one
- c ☐ two hundred and one

b ▶ 10.01 Listen and check.

c Write the numbers in words.

1. 85,000,000 *eighty-five million*
2. 379 ______________
3. 8,162 ______________
4. 450,000 ______________
5. 2009 ______________
6. 7,299,612 ______________

3 PRONUNCIATION Main stress

a ▶ 10.02 Listen and decide where the main stress is in each superlative form. Check (✓) the correct stress marking.

1 a ☐ English is the <u>most</u> popular language in the world.
  b ☑ English is the most <u>popular</u> language in the world.
2 a ☐ Suriname is one of the <u>small</u>est countries in South America.
  b ☐ Suriname is one of the small<u>est</u> countries in South America.
3 a ☐ This is one of the most <u>dangerous</u> cities in the world.
  b ☐ This is one of the <u>most</u> dangerous cities in the world.
4 a ☐ Brazil is the bigg<u>est</u> country in Latin America.
  b ☐ Brazil is the <u>bigg</u>est country in Latin America.
5 a ☐ Spanish is one of the most <u>useful</u> languages in the world.
  b ☐ Spanish is one of the <u>most</u> useful languages in the world.
6 a ☐ This is the <u>most</u> expensive hotel in the city.
  b ☐ This is the most <u>expensive</u> hotel in the city.
7 a ☐ This is one of the <u>sadd</u>est movies ever.
  b ☐ This is one of the sadd<u>est</u> movies ever.
8 a ☐ This is the heavi<u>est</u> thing in my bag.
  b ☐ This is the <u>hea</u>viest thing in my bag.

10C EVERYDAY ENGLISH
There's something I don't know how to do

1 USEFUL LANGUAGE
Asking for help

a Complete the conversation with the words in the box.

showing not at all like this right ~~could~~
looks so first of course easy

A 1 *Could* you help me with something?
B Yes, 2 ____________. What is it?
A I don't know how to record shows on my new TV.
B Sure, that's 3 ____________.
A Would you mind 4 ____________ me?
B No, 5 ____________. So, what you do is this. First you go to the program menu, then you find the show you want, and finally you press "Record."
A OK, that 6 ____________ easy. Now let me try. 7 ____________ I go to the program menu?
B Yes, that's right.
A Then I find the show I want with these arrows, 8 ____________?
B Correct.
A And then I just press the "Record" button. Is that 9 ____________?
B Yes, perfect.

b 10.03 Listen and check.

c Underline the correct words to complete the sentences.

1 **A** Could you *helping / to help / <u>help</u>* me with my homework?
  B Yes, *of course / off course / course.*
2 Can you explain *me / that to me / that me?*
3 **A** Would you mind *help / helping / to help* me?
  B No, *not at all / not all / no at all.*
4 **A** Do you mind *show / to show / showing* me how to take photos with my phone?
  B *Not problem / No problem / Without a problem.*
5 *At first / First place / So first* I click on this link?
6 Next I put in my password, *like this / as this / like these?*
7 And then I press this button. Is that *in right / right / on the right?*

d 10.04 Listen and check.

2 PRONUNCIATION
Main stress and intonation

a 10.05 Listen to the questions. Check (✓) the stressed word in each sentence.

1 Can you help me with something?
  a ☐ can
  b ☑ help
2 Would you mind showing me how to do it?
  a ☐ showing
  b ☐ mind
3 Could you explain that again, please?
  a ☐ could
  b ☐ explain
4 Do you mind helping me with my shopping?
  a ☐ helping
  b ☐ mind

b 10.06 Listen to the questions. Put a check (✓) to show if the intonation goes up (↗) or down (↘) at the end.

	↗	↘
1 How do I check my email?	☐	☑
2 Can you show me how to log in?	☐	☐
3 What's the problem with your computer?	☐	☐
4 Would you mind speaking more slowly, please?	☐	☐
5 Do you mind showing me how to take photos?	☐	☐
6 How often do you check your email?	☐	☐

10D SKILLS FOR WRITING
My friends send really funny texts

1 READING

a On "Compare the Web" you can compare different websites. Read people's opinions about two social media sites, Interfriends and BestiesLink. Who thinks these things? Use the names in the box.

Joe K	~~Enuff!~~	Helpme2	Lizzie39

1 I use the site to help me with my studies. Enuff!
2 My friends and I enjoy photography. ______
3 Social media isn't the best way to talk to people. ______
4 It's the best site to make plans with friends. ______

b Read the opinions again. Are the sentences true or false?

1 Joe K is quiet and doesn't like spending time with his friends.
2 Enuff! is a bad language student and never studies.
3 Helpme2 doesn't use social media very often.
4 Lizzie39 thinks social media sites are a bad idea.
5 More people prefer Interfriends to BestiesLink.

For me, Interfriends is better than BestiesLink. You can put a lot of pictures on Interfriends and make bigger photo albums. Most of my friends use Interfriends as well, so it's easier to talk to them. We like to plan events and parties in group chats.

Joe K Like | Reply | Share

BestiesLink is the most famous social media site in my country, so of course it's the best. You can do more things on it, too. It's also a good site because you can use different apps on it. For example, my friends and I use a language learning app and study English together.

Enuff! Like | Reply | Share

I use Interfriends almost every day. It's quicker to share photos with friends than on BestiesLink, and I love taking pictures.

Helpme2 Like | Reply | Share

I don't like Interfriends or BestiesLink. If I want to talk to my friends or show them photos, I can go to their house. My real friends are better than some people I only see on social media sites.

Lizzie39 Like | Reply | Share

2 WRITING SKILLS Linking ideas with *also*, *too*, and *as well*

a Rewrite the sentences. Add the words in parentheses in the correct places.

1 He speaks Chinese perfectly and he speaks a little Japanese. (too)
He speaks Chinese perfectly and he speaks a little Japanese, too.
2 My new tablet is smaller than my old laptop. It's lighter, so it's easier to carry. (also)
______
3 Put in your username and enter your password. (as well)
______
4 I can take great photos with my new phone, and I can post them on social media. (also)
______
5 He has a new tablet and a new smartphone. (too)
______
6 My uncle gave me a laptop and he bought me a printer. (as well)
______

3 WRITING

a Think of two websites you use that are similar. Write a post comparing them on "Compare the Web." Look at Joe K's post to help you. Remember to:

- say why you like one more than the other
- say what you use the better site for and why
- use also, too, and as well.

For me, ______ is better than ______

Like | Reply | Share

UNIT 10
Reading and listening extension

1 READING

a Read the text. Complete each sentence with the correct tip number.

1 Tip 5 talks about doing something for the first time.
2 Tip ___ talks about staying healthy.
3 Tip ___ talks about spending less time on your phone.
4 Tip ___ talks about spending time with the people who are important to you.
5 Tip ___ talks about being friendly.

b Read the text again. Match 1–8 with a–h to make sentences.

1 [g] Checking emails often takes
2 [ ] Getting in shape can help
3 [ ] Doing exercise is
4 [ ] It's important not to forget
5 [ ] Many of us spend
6 [ ] It's a good idea to
7 [ ] When you are nice to other people,
8 [ ] Helping other people

a a lot of time on social media.
b about your family and friends.
c can be good for you.
d try new and different things sometimes.
e good for your brain.
f they are usually nice to you.
g too much of our time.
h you to feel happier.

c What other things do you think are important for a happy life? Write some more tips. Remember to write:

- what the tip is
- how often someone should do this
- how it will make them feel better.

Tired? Bored? Feel like you could be happier?

If that's you, read our top five tips for a better life.

1 Get some exercise. Most people feel happier when they're in shape. And did you know that going for a walk is better for your brain than playing chess or doing puzzles? A stronger body means a stronger brain, too!

2 Make plans with a friend! When we're busy, we can sometimes forget about our family and friends. But they're the most important people to us. Spend some time with someone you don't talk to enough at least once a week.

3 Spend less time on your phone. Check your email once a day – twice if you really have to – but not twenty times! And think about how much time you spend on social media – if you're like most people, it's too much.

4 Do something for other people! We know that people who help others are healthier and happier than those who don't. And remember: people will be friendlier and nicer to you if you're friendly and nice to them! Smile at the bus driver or the salesperson, and watch them smile back at you.

5 Try something new! Did you ever think of learning a language, trying a new sport, or playing the piano? Well, don't just think about it – do it! It's probably easier than you think.

For more ideas, visit our website.

2 LISTENING

a ▶10.07 Listen to the podcast. Check (✓) the best description of what the person says.

1 ☐ People who live in Blue Zones live longer and are near oceans, rivers, and lakes.
2 ☐ People who live in Blue Zones live longer and eat a lot of meat.
3 ☐ People who live in Blue Zones live longer and do some exercise.

b Complete the sentences about the podcast. Use numbers (e.g., *300*), not words (e.g., *three hundred*).

1 In 2019, there were about ___*80,000*___ people over 100.
2 In 2014, there were ______________ Americans aged 100 or older.
3 Blue Zones are places that have the highest number of people ______________ years old or older.
4 Both coffee and tea drinkers are in ______________ percent less danger of an early death.
5 Keep a healthy social network. This can help you live up to ______________ percent longer.
6 ______________ close friends in your social network may lower the danger of early death.

c ▶10.07 Listen to the podcast again. Are the sentences true or false?

1 The number of Americans 100 years old is bigger now.
2 The people who live in Loma Linda eat sugar, dance, and watch TV.
3 The people in Costa Rica feel good about life.
4 Okinawa is the home of the world's oldest men.
5 Eight hours is not enough sleep.

Review and extension

1 GRAMMAR

Correct the sentences.

1 My new computer is more fast than my old one.
My new computer is faster than my old one.
2 Tablets are usually lighter that laptops.
3 London is the most big city in the U.K.
4 This hotel is cheapper than the Hotel Classic.
5 It's the more expensive restaurant in the world.
6 Spanish is more easy to learn than Navajo.
7 English is the most useful language of the world.
8 I'm not very good at math, but Ian is badder than me.

2 VOCABULARY

Correct the sentences.

1 There was nothing good on TV, so I go on social media after dinner.
There was nothing good on TV, so I went on social media after dinner.
2 I use my smartphone to do calls to my family and friends.
3 I online to check the weather.
4 You need my password to log to my computer.
5 Press "Control" and "S" when you want to safe your document.
6 It's taking a long time to inload the file from this website.

3 WORDPOWER *most*

Choose the correct words to complete the sentences.

1 I felt sick yesterday, so I was in bed *most day* / <u>*most of the day*</u> / *most of day*.
2 They love watching all kinds of sports, but they like tennis *most of all* / *most all* / *most everything*.
3 *Most friends mine* / *Most my friends* / *Most of my friends* live in Brazil.
4 I think *most people* / *most the people* / *most of people* like listening to music.
5 *Most the students* / *Most of the students* / *Most of students* in my class speak excellent English.
6 We visit my grandparents *most of Sundays* / *most of the Sundays* / *most Sundays*.

REVIEW YOUR PROGRESS

Look again at Review Your Progress on p. 108 of the Student's Book. How well can you do these things now?
3 = very well 2 = well 1 = not so well

I CAN ...	
compare and talk about things I have	☐
talk about languages	☐
ask for help	☐
write a post expressing an opinion.	☐

11A I'VE HEARD SHE'S A GOOD ACTRESS

1 GRAMMAR Present perfect

a Complete the sentences with the present perfect form of the verbs in the box.

see go act do try read dance ~~meet~~

1 Have you ever met a famous soccer player?
2 Gina __________ __________ the movie *Avengers: Endgame* eight times!
3 David and Max __________ never __________ any of the Harry Potter books.
4 No, he __________ __________ in a Shakespeare play before.
5 We __________ never __________ Japanese food.
6 I __________ never __________ the tango before.
7 No, I __________ __________ a bungee jump before, so I'm really nervous.
8 __________ your mother ever __________ to Australia or New Zealand?

b Put the words in the correct order to make sentences.

1 ever / have / heard of / you / the Spanish actress / Paz Vega ?
Have you ever heard of the Spanish actress, Paz Vega?
2 won / never / Tom Cruise / has / an Oscar .
____
3 written / has / ever / she / any songs / in French ?
____
4 to Canada / we / been / have / before / never .
____
5 in an orchestra / ever / have / Mel and Tom / played ?
____
6 never / I / have / before / a movie star / met .
____
7 had / you / have / a birthday party / ever / in a restaurant ?
____
8 the Tower of London / have / never / they / visited .
____

2 VOCABULARY Irregular past participles

a Find the irregular past participles for the verbs in the box.

~~see~~ win eat have break catch meet do hear buy make steal write read

Q	H	X	E	N	I	S	F	G	B	D	E	F	G	L
H	Z	F	B	F	H	J	K	E	R	E	A	X	G	K
H	F	M	X	E	J	L	R	Z	O	S	W	R	R	C
E	A	T	E	N	A	N	E	M	K	S	O	G	N	A
A	I	A	H	B	C	D	A	S	E	G	N	N	S	U
R	F	B	F	G	H	A	D	D	N	N	G	S	D	G
D	F	P	R	W	E	F	H	V	F	D	S	U	U	H
B	G	D	Y	O	Y	U	F	B	J	S	S	D	F	T
F	E	H	O	I	A	D	H	J	V	T	V	E	G	G
H	S	E	E	N	P	D	F	B	B	O	U	G	H	T
P	H	H	G	F	E	M	A	G	N	L	K	D	V	R
D	H	L	Y	U	U	A	Q	D	F	E	L	F	D	A
S	Z	A	A	L	O	D	W	D	F	N	R	M	Z	I
F	W	R	I	T	T	E	N	F	G	H	D	D	E	Q
U	T	T	D	F	J	N	G	S	X	U	X	Q	E	T

b Complete the past participles in the sentences.

1 Have you ever been to Spain?
2 *The Godfather* is the best movie I've ever s__________.
3 I've never w__________ a competition.
4 My brother's b__________ his arm three times.

5 Have you ever e__________ an unusual dish?
6 He's w__________ a lot of magazine articles.
7 My father has r__________ hundreds of books. He's very smart.
8 We've never b__________ a house.

3 PRONUNCIATION Sentence stress

a 11.01 Listen to the sentences and check (✓) the correct stress marking.

1 a ☐ <u>I've</u> never read any novels by Ernest Hemingway.
b ☑ I've never <u>read</u> any novels by Ernest Hemingway.
2 a ☐ <u>Have</u> you ever stayed in that hotel?
b ☐ Have you ever <u>stayed</u> in that hotel?
3 a ☐ He's <u>driven</u> to Charleston six times this year.
b ☐ <u>He's</u> driven to Charleston six times this year.
4 a ☐ Ella and Greg have never <u>met</u> you.
b ☐ Ella and Greg <u>have</u> never met you.
5 a ☐ <u>Have</u> you ever bought a new car?
b ☐ Have you ever <u>bought</u> a new car?
6 a ☐ She hasn't <u>met</u> the president before.
b ☐ She <u>hasn't</u> met the president before.

11B I BET YOU'VE NEVER BEEN TO THE OPERA

1 GRAMMAR Present perfect or simple past

a Match questions 1–6 with answers a–f.

1 [e] Has he ever won an Oscar?
2 [ ] Did you go on vacation last year?
3 [ ] How many times have you visited New York?
4 [ ] Did you do anything special this weekend?
5 [ ] Have they ever been to a musical on Broadway?
6 [ ] Did she enjoy her birthday party?

a I've only been there once, in 2015.
b No, not really. We just went out for a pizza on Saturday night.
c Yes, they have, actually. They saw *Hamilton* when they were in New York last year.
d Yes, she did. She had a fantastic time.
e Yes, he has. He got one for the movie *Bohemian Rhapsody* in 2019.
f Yes, we did. We went to Cancún in Mexico.

b Underline the correct words to complete the conversation.

A 1 *Have you ever been / Did you ever go* to London?
B Yes, I 2 *have / did*. I 3 *'ve stayed / stayed* there lots of times on business.
A 4 *Have you ever seen / Did you ever see* any musicals in the West End?
B No, I 5 *didn't / haven't*. However, I 6 *went / 've been* to the theater a few times.
A Really? What 7 *have you seen / did you see* the last time you went?
B I 8 *saw / have seen* Shakespeare's *Romeo and Juliet* at The Globe Theatre last summer.
A Who 9 *have you been / did you go* with?
B I 10 *went / have been* with some British friends.
A 11 *Have you enjoyed it / Did you enjoy it?*
B Yes, I 12 *have / did*. The acting 13 *was / has been* great!

2 VOCABULARY Music

a Underline the correct words to match the pictures.

1 *a DJ / a musician*

2 *an opera singer / a pop singer*

3 *a classical dancer / a jazz musician*

4 *a rock band / a classical orchestra*

5 *tango DJs / tango dancers*

6 *a rock band / an opera*

b Complete the sentences.

1 Rudolf Nureyev was a famous ballet dancer in the 1960s and 1970s.
2 I think Pavarotti was the best opera ________ of his generation.
3 He's an amazing ________. He can play the piano, the guitar, and the cello.
4 Anna's a violinist in one of the best-known ________ in the U.S.
5 He thinks U2 is the most famous rock ________ that Ireland has ever produced.
6 My parents love ________ music, especially Beethoven and Tchaikovsky.
7 My grandfather loved ________ music. His favorite singer was Bob Dylan.
8 On the radio, they usually play ________ music by artists like Lady Gaga and Ariana Grande.
9 Louis Armstrong was a popular ________ singer. He also played the trumpet.
10 The Rolling Stones is one of the most famous ________ bands in the world.

3 PRONUNCIATION Syllables

a 11.02 Listen to the sentences. Which syllable is stressed in the **bold** words? Check (✓) the correct stress marking.

1 He's a great **actor**.
a [ ] actor
b [✓] actor

2 She's a famous Hollywood movie **director**.
a [ ] director
b [ ] director

3 I went to the **theater** in London last night.
a [ ] theater
b [ ] theater

4 She was a well-known **model** when she was young.
a [ ] model
b [ ] model

5 I'd like to be a fashion **photographer**.
a [ ] photographer
b [ ] photographer

6 She's won several **national** prizes.
a [ ] national
b [ ] national

7 He's the best **musician** in our family.
a [ ] musician
b [ ] musician

8 The **orchestra** played for three hours.
a [ ] orchestra
b [ ] orchestra

11C EVERYDAY ENGLISH
I thought they were really good

1 USEFUL LANGUAGE
Asking for and expressing opinions

a Complete the conversation with the sentences in the box.

Yes, I thought it was great.
No, me neither. Anyway, let's go get coffee.
~~I really liked the movie. How about you?~~
Really? I thought the music was fine. Also, I thought the photography was great.
Yeah, maybe.

TIM So what did you think of the movie?
SAM 1 I really liked the movie. How about you?
TIM I thought it was pretty good, but it was kind of long.
SAM 2 ____________
TIM Did you like the music?
SAM 3 ____________
TIM You did? I thought it was kind of loud. Sometimes I couldn't hear the actors very well.
SAM 4 ____________
TIM Yes, me too. But I didn't like the actor who played Nelson Mandela.
SAM 5 ____________

b 11.03 Listen and check.

c Correct the sentences.

1 **A** What have you thought of the concert?
What did you think of the concert?
B I really like it.
2 **A** Did you enjoyed the movie?
B Yes, I was. I thinked the acting was excellent.
3 **A** I didn't like very much the singer.
B Me, too.
4 **A** I've thought the music was beautiful.
B Yes, me also.
5 **A** I have really enjoyed the concert last night. How are you?
B I haven't liked the first half at all, but the second half has been amazing.

2 PRONUNCIATION
Main stress and intonation

a 11.04 Listen to the short conversations. Put a check (✓) to show if B's responses go up (↗) or down (↘).

		↗	↘
1 **A** I thought the movie was great.	**B** You did?	✓	☐
2 **A** I really liked the music.	**B** Me too.	☐	☐
3 **A** I love going to the theater.	**B** You do?	☐	☐
4 **A** I didn't like Samuel L. Jackson's last movie.	**B** Me neither.	☐	☐

11D SKILLS FOR WRITING
It was an interesting movie

1 READING

a Mariusz, from Poland, and Ariel, from Argentina, both went to see the band Flags in their hometowns. Read their messages to each other about the concerts and check (✓) the correct answers.

1 Who thought the concert was terrible?
a ☐ Mariusz b ☐ Ariel
2 Who thought the concert was really good?
a ☐ Mariusz b ☐ Ariel

Hi Ariel,

How are you? I hope your family is well.

I wanted to write and tell you about the Flags concert I went to last weekend. It was fantastic! I loved every minute of it. I went with a big group of friends from college. It was really crazy, but a lot of fun! The lead singer had an amazing voice, and the band played all their songs. The singers in the band talked to everyone, too. They were really nice and very friendly. I'd love to see them again.

If you visit me in Poland next year, maybe we can go and see them on their next tour. What do you think?

See you,

Mariusz

Hey Mariusz,

Great to hear from you! My family and I are all well. Thanks for asking. Come and visit us again any time!

So, you really liked the Flags concert? I'm surprised. I saw them at the stadium here in Mendoza a few months ago, and I didn't like them at all. I went with my sister for her birthday. (She really likes the lead singer!) I thought the music was terrible. It was too loud!

And when the band talked to the crowd, it was so boring. I didn't go to a concert to listen to four men talking! Thanks for the invitation, but I don't want to see them again!

When I visit you in Poland, we can see a different band that we both like!

See you,

Ariel

b Read the messages again. Are the sentences true or false?

1 Mariusz went to the concert with his family.
2 Flags played all their songs at the concert Mariusz went to.
3 The band only played music at the concerts.
4 Flags sang at the concert hall in Ariel's town.
5 Ariel doesn't want to see Flags with Mariusz.

2 WRITING SKILLS Object pronouns

a Rewrite the sentences. Change the **bold** words to object pronouns to avoid repetition.

1 I read Jane Austen's *Emma* last week. I really loved **Jane Austen's *Emma***.
I read Jane Austen's *Emma* last week. I really loved it.
2 Daniel Radcliffe was my favorite actor in the movie. **Daniel Radcliffe** was really good.
3 We want to see the new Studio Ghibli movie. My friend, Andy, told us **the new Studio Ghibli movie** is amazing.
4 Alfonso Cuarón is a fantastic director. **Alfonso Cuarón** won an Oscar for the movie *Roma*.
5 I thought Jay-Z and Beyoncé were fantastic in concert. **Jay-Z and Beyoncé** are both great musicians.

3 WRITING

a Think of a concert you've been to, a movie you've seen, or a book you've read. Write a message to a friend with your opinions about it. Remember to write:

- when you went / saw it / read it
- if you liked it
- your opinions about the singer / actor / main character, etc.
- if you recommend it.

UNIT 11
Reading and listening extension

1 READING

a Read the text and underline the correct words to complete the sentences.

1 Lisa Kudrow *works* / *worked* as a scientist.
2 Lisa studied *biology* / *acting* in college.
3 Lisa was *a producer* / *an* actor on the show *Friends*.
4 Lisa and her husband have a *son* / *daughter*.
5 Lisa is / *was* an actor, writer, and producer.

b Read the text again. Complete the sentences with the correct forms of the verbs in the box.

~~play~~ win study be earn live act

1 Lisa Kudrow played tennis in high school.
2 Lisa and Michel ________ in Los Angeles now.
3 She ________ in many popular TV shows.
4 Lisa ________ biology in college.
5 The actors ________ a lot of money for working on *Friends*.
6 Lisa ________ an actor for many years.
7 She ________ awards for her excellent work in TV shows and movies.

c Write a profile of a famous person. Make sure you include at least three verbs in the present perfect form.

Celebrity Profile

Lisa Kudrow is a famous actor who has won several awards, including an Emmy. She has played some great characters on TV shows and in movies, but she hasn't always been an actor. Before she became a famous actor, Lisa was an athlete and a scientist.

Lisa grew up in California. When she was in high school, Lisa was a great student and an excellent tennis player. Her father was a doctor who helped people with headaches, and her mother was a travel agent. Lisa went to college in New York and earned a biology degree. After college, she worked as a medical researcher for her father.

Lisa left her job and soon got the role of Phoebe Buffay in the popular TV show *Friends*. The show became so famous that Lisa and her co-stars earned over $1 million for each episode! She became a big star and has acted in many movies and TV shows since *Friends*. She is also a writer and a producer. She has worked as a producer for TV shows like *Who Do You Think You Are?* and *Web Therapy*.

Lisa lives in Los Angeles. She married Michel Stern in 1995, and they had a son named Julian in 1998. Since Julian was born, Lisa has acted in several movies for children, such as *Hotel for Dogs* and *The Boss Baby*. Lisa Kudrow is a very smart superstar who has had an amazing life!

2 LISTENING

a 11.05 Listen to the conversation. Check (✓) the things Marianne and Lenny talk about.

☐ places they have been to	☐ food they have eaten
☐ famous people they have met	☐ movies they have seen
☐ stories they have read	☐ music they enjoy

b 11.05 Listen to the conversation again and check (✓) the correct answers.

1 Why does Lenny like Mexico?
- a ☐ He likes the history, the music, and the food.
- b ☑ He likes the history, the beaches, and the food.
- c ☐ He likes the history, the beaches, and the weather.

2 Why doesn't Marianne want to try Mexican food?
- a ☐ She doesn't eat meat.
- b ☐ She doesn't like beans.
- c ☐ She's never been to Mexico.

3 Why does Marianne like Bologna so much?
- a ☐ She met Lenny there.
- b ☐ She's seen operas there.
- c ☐ She's had good food there.

4 How much Italian does Marianne speak?
- a ☐ A lot. She learned it at school.
- b ☐ None. She's forgotten all of it.
- c ☐ Not much. She's forgotten most of it.

5 What has Marianne seen in Milan?
- a ☐ Italian operas
- b ☐ pop singers
- c ☐ classical music concerts

6 Why does Marianne already know about the band Arctic Fire?
- a ☐ Because she went to one of their concerts.
- b ☐ Because her brother has some of their albums.
- c ☐ Because her friend in Italy likes them.

7 What does Marianne think you need to do to enjoy classical music?
- a ☐ Go to concerts.
- b ☐ Listen to it more than one time.
- c ☐ Like different kinds of music.

8 What often happens when Lenny buys pop albums?
- a ☐ He likes one song best at first, and it stays his favorite song.
- b ☐ When he has listened several times, he gets bored with it.
- c ☐ He likes one song best at first, then starts to like other songs more.

c Write about the things you enjoy in your life. Start with these topics and add two of your own:

- What's the best food you've eaten?
- What's the most interesting place you've been?
- What's the best present anyone has bought for you?

For each topic, describe the thing you have chosen and explain why you liked it.

Review and extension

1 GRAMMAR

Correct the sentences.

1 Have you never met a famous pop singer?
Have you ever met a famous pop singer?
2 I never seen a movie by Quentin Tarantino.
3 They has never been to Barcelona.
4 I haven't never been to France on vacation.
5 My uncle has write lots of children's books.
6 Have ever you read any of the Harry Potter books?
7 **A** Has he ever been to Scotland?
B No, he never.
8 I'm visited my grandmother three times this week.

2 VOCABULARY

Correct the sentences.

1 My dad's ben to Colombia seven times.
My dad's been to Colombia seven times.
2 I've never forgetted your birthday.
3 No, I've never flied in a helicopter.
4 Have they maken a new James Bond film?
5 I've taked lots of photos of the party.
6 No, I've never takken the bus to school. I always walk.

3 WORDPOWER *Multi-word verbs*

Complete the sentences with the multi-word verbs. Use one word from each line.

come try grew call fill ~~lies~~
over on ~~down~~ up back in

1 My father always *lies* *down* on the sofa when he's watching TV. He usually falls asleep.
2 I ______ ______ in Canada, but I went to college in Paris.
3 Sorry, he isn't here right now. I'll ask him to ______ you ______.
4 If you ______ ______ at about 8:00, we can watch the soccer game on my new 3D TV.
5 If you want to join the gym, first you have to ______ ______ this application form.
6 Why don't you ______ these jeans ______?

REVIEW YOUR PROGRESS

Look again at Review Your Progress on p. 118 of the Student's Book. How well can you do these things now?
3 = very well 2 = well 1 = not so well

I CAN ...	
ask and answer about entertainment experiences	☐
talk about events I've been to	☐
express opinions about things I've seen	☐
write a review.	☐

12A WHAT ARE YOU GOING TO DO?

1 VOCABULARY Geography

a Complete the crossword puzzle.

→ Across

3 The Amazon is the longest __river__ in South America.
6 Scientists are very worried about the animals and trees in the Amazon ________ in Brazil.
8 A ________ is a huge area of ice millions of years old that moves very slowly down a mountain valley.
9 When I go on vacation to the coast, I don't like lying on the ________ all day.
10 A ________ is a large body of fresh water with land all around it.

↓ Down

1 Cuba is one of the largest ________ in the Caribbean.
2 The sequoias are the largest trees in the world, and you can see them in a huge ________ in California.
4 Angel Falls is one of the highest ________ in the world.
5 Everest is the tallest ________ in the world.
7 Death Valley is in the Mojave ________ in Eastern California. It is one of the hottest places on Earth.

2 GRAMMAR *be going to*

a Match questions 1–6 with answers a–f.

1 [e] Are you going to stay in a hotel?
2 [ ] What are you going to do in Venezuela?
3 [ ] Is she going to go to college next year?
4 [ ] How are you going to save enough money to travel?
5 [ ] Are they going to stay with their uncle in California?
6 [ ] Are you going to catch the bus to the airport?

a No, she isn't going to continue studying. She's going to get a job as an English teacher in Mexico.
b We're going to work in a big hotel in New York City for six months.
c Yes, they are. He's going to get them a job in a restaurant in San Francisco.
d No, we aren't. We're going to call a taxi at about 4 o'clock.
e No, we aren't. We're going to go camping.
f We're going to go hiking in the mountains.

b Complete the sentences with the verbs in the box and the correct form of *be going to*. Use contractions where possible.

visit	(not) go	stay	look	(not) take	come	~~do~~	have

1 What __are__ you __going to do__ this weekend?
2 He ________ a vacation this year because he bought a new car.
3 We ________ the Sydney Opera House while we're in Australia.
4 Which hotel ________ you ________ at when you're in Chicago?
5 ________ she ________ for a job in San Antonio?
6 ________ you ________ a big party for your thirtieth birthday?
7 I ________ to the beach this afternoon. It looks like it's going to rain.
8 They ________ over to watch the World Cup on TV with us this evening.

3 PRONUNCIATION Syllables and word stress

a 12.01 Listen to the sentences. Which syllable is stressed in the **bold** words? Check (✓) the correct stress marking.

1 In Hawaii, the **accommodations** are really expensive.
a [ ] accommo**da**tions b [ ] ac**com**modations
2 I've done a lot of **sightseeing** today.
a [ ] sight**see**ing b [ ] **sight**seeing
3 I like living in the **countryside**.
a [ ] **coun**tryside b [ ] country**side**
4 We have a **reservation** for 7:30.
a [ ] reserva**tion** b [ ] reser**va**tion
5 The **nightlife** in Mexico City was fantastic.
a [ ] **night**life b [ ] night**life**
6 I love **traveling** to different countries.
a [ ] **tra**veling b [ ] trave**ling**
7 That **restaurant** has fantastic food.
a [ ] restau**rant** b [ ] **res**taurant
8 The **scenery** in Brazil was amazing.
a [ ] **sce**nery b [ ] sce**ne**ry

12B YOU SHOULD LIVE LIKE THE LOCAL PEOPLE

1 GRAMMAR *should / shouldn't*

a Underline the best words to complete the sentences.

1 You *should / shouldn't* do some research before you go, so you know the best places to visit.
2 You *should / shouldn't* change your money at the airport. It's better to change it at a bank.
3 You *should / shouldn't* call your parents every two or three days, so they know you're safe.
4 You *should / shouldn't* book some accommodations before you travel. Hotels are often full this time of the year.
5 You *should / shouldn't* speak too loudly to the local people. They might think it's rude.
6 You *should / shouldn't* learn some useful expressions in the local language. People like it when visitors can say a few words in their language.
7 You *should / shouldn't* spend too much time in the sun. It's very strong at this time of the year.
8 You *should / shouldn't* carry a lot of cash with you. It's safer to get money from ATMs when you need it.

b Correct the sentences.

1 You shouldn't to take so many jeans with you on vacation.
You shouldn't take so many jeans with you on vacation.
2 She don't should walk home alone. It's safer to go by taxi.
______
3 You should seeing the new James Bond movie. It's amazing!
______
4 Where I should change my money?
______
5 Which countries do I should visit in South America?
______
6 My dad thinks I should going to college next year.
______
7 They should to go to the Gold Museum when they're in Colombia.
______
8 I should invite Selena and her sister to the party?
______

2 VOCABULARY Travel collocations

a Match 1–6 with a–f to make sentences.

1 [c] The first thing I do when I get to my hotel is to unpack
2 [ ] Elena and Carla are making
3 [ ] During vacations, my wife prefers to stay in
4 [ ] I think teachers are very lucky because they can often take
5 [ ] We don't have enough money for a vacation this year, so we're going to stay
6 [ ] I think you should live

a hotels, but I think it's more fun to go camping.
b home and invite some friends to come and stay with us.
c my suitcase and put all my clothes in the wardrobe.
d abroad if you want to learn to speak a foreign language well.
e plans to travel around Asia for six months.
f a long summer vacation.

b Complete the sentences with the correct forms of the verbs in the box.

plan stay ~~change~~ book travel pack

1 She says she can't come to the party tonight because she had to <u>change</u> her plans.
2 I ______ a vacation to California, but I couldn't go because of my sister's wedding.
3 It always takes her about six hours to ______ her bags before she goes on vacation.
4 We ______ the hotel in January, but now they say we don't have a reservation.
5 He usually ______ abroad six or seven times a year.
6 There weren't any flights to Washington, D.C. that day because the weather was bad, so they ______ home.

12C EVERYDAY ENGLISH
Is breakfast included?

1 USEFUL LANGUAGE
Checking in at a hotel; Asking for tourist information

a Put the conversation between a guest (G) and a hotel receptionist (R) in the correct order.

- ☐ **G** Henderson.
- ☐ **G** What time is breakfast?
- ☐ **R** Yes, there is. It's on the top floor next to the spa.
- 1 **R** Hello. How can I help you?
- ☐ **G** And what time is check-out?
- ☐ **R** It's from 7:00 until 10:00 in the dining room.
- ☐ **G** Thanks.
- ☐ **G** I have a reservation for three nights.
- ☐ **G** Oh, and one last thing. Is there a gym I can use?
- ☐ **R** It's free of charge for our guests.
- ☐ **R** It's 12 o'clock on the day you leave.
- ☐ **R** So here's your key. Enjoy your stay.
- ☐ **R** Three nights? Your name, please?
- ☐ **R** Thank you. Yes, that's right … Henderson. Three nights.
- ☐ **G** How much does it cost to use the gym?
- ☐ **G** OK, that's great.

b Match sentences 1–8 with responses a–h.

1 *e* I won a weekend in the Bahamas!
2 ☐ Can I buy tickets here?
3 ☐ Is breakfast included?
4 ☐ I saw Brad Pitt in a café yesterday!
5 ☐ Could I have four tickets, please?
6 ☐ Can I pay by credit card?
7 ☐ She's going to get her husband a cat for his birthday.
8 ☐ How much is it for a ticket?

a It's $10 for adults and $6 for children.
b Sure. That's $32, please.
c No problem. Please insert your card here.
d Oh, really? I didn't know Sean liked animals.
e You did? Wow! That's fantastic!
f You did? Did you talk to him?
g Yes, it is. It's from 6:30 to 9:30 in the restaurant.
h Yes, you can. They're $20 each.

2 PRONUNCIATION
Intonation to show surprise

a 12.02 Listen to the short conversations. Put a check (✓) to show if B's responses go up (↗) or down (↘).

			↗	↘
1	**A**	I won $1,000!		
	B	Really?	✓	☐
2	**A**	Thanks for all your help.		
	B	No problem.	☐	☐
3	**A**	I'm hungry.		
	B	Me too. When's breakfast?	☐	☐
4	**A**	I missed the last train.		
	B	You did?	☐	☐
5	**A**	I went to Philadelphia for the weekend.		
	B	You did?	☐	☐
6	**A**	Can you call me a taxi, please?		
	B	Of course.	☐	☐
7	**A**	There's a parking lot under the hotel.		
	B	How much is it?	☐	☐
8	**A**	She's going to live in the U.S.		
	B	She is?	☐	☐
9	**A**	I really like opera.		
	B	You do?	☐	☐
10	**A**	There's a really good café near my house.		
	B	What time does it open?	☐	☐

12D SKILLS FOR WRITING

You should go to Stanley Park

1 READING

a Read Antonio and Gianni's emails and check (✓) the best answer.

1 ☐ Antonio and Ana are going to go to Florence for a short vacation.
2 ☐ Antonio is going to stay at Gianni's house in Florence.
3 ☐ Antonio wants some information about where he should go in Florence.
4 ☐ Antonio has visited Florence before.

b Read the emails again. Are the sentences true or false?

1 Antonio wants to know about interesting places to visit and good places to eat.
2 *Il Ponte Vecchio* is the name of an expensive shop in Florence.
3 The statue of *David* is in the Uffizi Gallery.
4 The *Piazza della Signoria* is a great place to have coffee.
5 Gianni doesn't like the food at *Il Santo Bevitore.*
6 Gianni would like to meet Antonio while he is in Florence.

Hi Gianni,

My name is Antonio, and my friend Ana said I should write to you. I'm going to come to Florence for a week in September. I've never been to Florence, so could you give me some advice about the best places to visit?

Also, I'd like to try some typical Italian food while I'm in Florence. Could you recommend some good restaurants?

I hope you can help me.

Kind regards,
Antonio

Hi Antonio,

Thanks for your email. It's great that you're going to come to my hometown in September. I'm very happy to help you plan your vacation.

You asked me about places to visit in Florence, so here are some ideas. First, you should visit the old bridge. We call it *Il Ponte Vecchio*. It's in the historic center of Florence and there are lots of stores on the bridge where you can buy presents. The stores are pretty expensive, but it's a beautiful place to begin a tour of Florence. Secondly, you should go to the Accademia Gallery. Here you can see Michelangelo's *David*. It's one of the most famous statues in the world. Finally, the third place you should go to is the Uffizi Gallery. It has an amazing collection of Renaissance paintings. It's near a beautiful square called the *Piazza della Signoria*. There are some nice cafés in the square where you can enjoy an excellent cup of Italian coffee.

You also asked me about restaurants. My favorite is *Il Santo Bevitore*. All the food there is fantastic!

I hope my ideas are useful. Maybe we can meet when you come to Florence!

Best wishes,

Gianni

2 WRITING SKILLS Paragraph writing

a Read the sentences. Put them in the correct order to make an email with an opening line, four paragraphs, and a closing line.

1 ☐ Secondly, you should go to the Royal Ontario Museum. It has an amazing collection of objects from all over the world.
2 ☐ I hope my ideas help you. Perhaps we can meet when you come to Toronto.
3 ☐ Thanks for your email.
4 ☐ You asked me about some interesting places to visit in Toronto, so here are some ideas.
5 ☐ Finally, the third place you should visit is the Art Gallery of Ontario. It is a great place to see paintings by Canadian artists.
6 ☐ You said you want to do some kind of sports activity. In December there are a lot of ice skating rinks in Toronto, so you can go ice skating. It's a lot of fun!
7 ☐ I'm pleased you're going to come to Toronto in December. I'm very happy to help you plan your trip.
8 ☐ Hi Edna,
9 ☐ Kind regards,
10 ☐ First, you should visit Casa Loma. It's a large castle with beautiful gardens.

3 WRITING

a Read Kenji's email and write a reply about a city or town you've visited. Think about:

- two or three places to visit
- why these places are interesting
- which places Kenji would like (read his email carefully)
- how to use paragraphs in your reply.

Hi ________, (your name)

My name is Kenji, and I'm going on vacation to ________ for a week in December. A friend of mine, Naoko, told me that you could give me some advice about the best places to visit in _______.

I'd like to do some sightseeing and go shopping while I'm there.

I hope you can help me.

Best wishes,
Kenji

UNIT 12
Reading and listening extension

1 READING

a Read the emails. Match 1–4 with a–d to make sentences.

1 [d] Sarah is busy because
2 [ ] Sarah asks Maggie
3 [ ] Maggie thinks Sarah and her sister
4 [ ] Maggie tells Sarah that

a shouldn't book a hotel.
b they should stay with friends.
c what she should plan for her sister.
d she is planning a vacation.

Hi Maggie,

How are you? Sorry I haven't written for a long time. I have been a little busy because I need to plan my vacation, but I have a problem.

The problem is that it's my sister's 25th birthday next month, and I want to do something special for her. I would really like to go on vacation abroad with her, but she often travels abroad for her work. So now she's bored with traveling and doesn't like staying in hotels. I don't want her to stay at home for her important birthday, but I don't know what kind of vacation to plan. Do you have any ideas?

Write soon and tell me how you're doing.

Sarah

b Read the emails again. Are these sentences true or false?

1 It is Sarah's birthday next month.
2 Sarah's sister wants to go on vacation and travel abroad.
3 Sarah wants to celebrate her sister's birthday abroad.
4 Maggie says that Sarah's sister should stay at home, if that's what she wants.
5 Maggie says that Sarah should plan a different kind of vacation.
6 Maggie would like to know what Sarah thinks of her idea.

c Write an email to a friend about a problem. For example:

- a problem with a friend
- a problem at work
- a problem about a vacation
- your own idea

d Write an email with an answer to the problem in c. Remember to write:

- what the person *should do*
- what the person *shouldn't do.*

From: Maggie
To: Sarah
Subject: Hello

Hi Sarah,

It's good to hear from you! I thought for a long time about your problem with your sister's birthday. Here's my idea – see what you think of it.

I think you should change your plans. You don't need to book a hotel to have a vacation. You just need to pack your sister's bag and find a list of her friends who live abroad. Then you make plans to visit all the people who have time to see you and that's it!

You shouldn't ask her if she wants to go. You should just do it! Your sister has probably forgotten that vacations aren't like work trips at all. When she remembers how much fun it is to visit her friends, she will never want to come back home again.

Write back soon and tell me what you think!

Maggie

2 LISTENING

a 12.03 Listen to the conversation. Complete the sentences.

1 Annette is going to buy an i*sland*________.
2 Stephanie thinks Annette should buy an island with nice b________.
3 Annette likes the place where her island is because she loves the c________.
4 From her island, you can see m________ and w________.

b 12.03 Listen to the conversation again and check (✓) the best endings for the sentences.

1 When Stephanie hears that Annette is buying an island, she is …
a ☐ angry.
b ☑ surprised.
2 Stephanie didn't know that people …
a ☐ sell islands.
b ☐ live on islands.
3 Annette is going to stay on the island …
a ☐ for vacations.
b ☐ for the whole year.
4 At the moment, there isn't a …
a ☐ tree on the island.
b ☐ house on the island.
5 The island that Annette has bought …
a ☐ is warm and sunny.
b ☐ has lovely views.
6 Annette and her family travel to the island …
a ☐ in someone else's boat.
b ☐ in their own boat.
7 Elena is going to …
a ☐ stay on the island with Annette and her family.
b ☐ stay on the island when Annette isn't there.
8 Elena can stay on the island …
a ☐ if she pays rent to Annette.
b ☐ for free because Annette is her friend.

c Write about things you are going to do in the future. Here are some possible ideas:

- live in a different place
- get a different job
- start a new hobby.

Your ideas don't have to be true!

Review

1 GRAMMAR

Correct the sentences.

1 We going to play tennis after school.
We're going to play tennis after school.
2 Are they go to have a party for David's birthday?
3 I go to go to college next year.
4 I'm going to shopping with my friends on Saturday.
5 Do you going to spend a week in Costa Rica?
6 She not going to study Economics in college.
7 We're going have dinner at a Greek restaurant tonight.
8 Greg going to go skiing in California in March. He's so lucky!

2 VOCABULARY

Correct the sentences.

1 In the afternoon, we took the ferry and visited an eyeland.
In the afternoon, we took the ferry and visited an island.
2 The country side is really beautiful.
3 The biggest waterfal in the U.S. is Niagara Falls.
4 The Sahara is one of the biggest desserts in the world.
5 You can see a lot of beautiful birds in the rain forest.
6 The tallest montains in South America are the Andes.
7 There were a lot of sheep in the feild behind the farm.
8 My dog loves swimming in the leik.

2 WORDPOWER *take*

Match 1–6 with a–f to make sentences.

1 [*d*] It took her
2 ☐ That road is dangerous. Please take
3 ☐ Flying is expensive, so they are going to take
4 ☐ Good morning, sir. Can I take
5 ☐ If you have a headache, you should take
6 ☐ The bus station? Yes, take

a the train to Vancouver. It's cheaper.
b the second left, and it's about 500 meters on the right.
c some aspirin.
d more than an hour to walk to the hotel.
e care when you walk across it.
f your bags to your room?

REVIEW YOUR PROGRESS

Look again at Review Your Progress on p. 128 of the Student's Book. How well can you do these things now?
3 = very well 2 = well 1 = not so well

I CAN …	
talk about vacation plans	☐
give advice	☐
talk about travel	☐
use language for travel and tourism	☐
write an email with travel advice.	☐

AUDIOSCRIPTS

Unit 1

01.01

Turkish
Irish
Japanese
Saudi
American
Russian
Mexican
Nigerian
Colombian

01.02

1 I like Jane. She's a warm and friendly person.
2 Our new teacher's really cool and he's very popular with his students.
3 Marisa's a fantastic singer. She's really well known in Portugal.
4 My friend Sarah's a wonderful person. She's really kind to all her friends.
5 Alicia is very quiet, but she's a great friend.
6 Mr. Jones is a very pleasant person and he's an amazing teacher.

01.03

chat
cake
keep
know
quiz
capital
bike
chart

01.04

1 How can I help you?
2 I'd like to take a fitness class.
3 What's your last name?
4 Can you spell that, please?
5 What time's the next class?
6 It's tomorrow at six thirty. / It's at six thirty tomorrow.
7 Where's the class?
8 It's in Room 3.
9 So that's 6:30 in Room 3?
10 Thanks for your help.
11 You're welcome.

01.05

A Hello. How can I help you?
B Hi. I'd like to take a German class. I'm a beginner.
A No problem. We have great German classes for beginners.
B When are the classes?
A They're on Mondays at 7:30.
B Great. I'm free on Monday evenings. Can I sign up for the class?
A Sure. What's your last name?
B Gonzales.
A Can you spell that, please?
B G-O-N-Z-A-L-E-S.
A Thank you. Enjoy the class.

01.06

1 Absolutely.
2 Good idea.
3 Me?
4 Sure.
5 Off to the gym?
6 Of course.
7 Is he from London?
8 Yes, he is.
9 Is she Argentinian?
10 No, she's not.
11 No problem.

01.07

1 three
2 eight
3 twelve
4 sixteen
5 right
6 match
7 brother
8 warm
9 kitchen
10 well known

01.08

CHARLIE Hi! Are you new to this soccer team?
PEDRO Yes. My name's Pedro.
C Hi, Pedro, I'm Charlie. Welcome to the team. Where are you from?
P I'm from Mazatlán, Mexico.
C Really? My grandma's Mexican. She's from Veracruz.
P Do you speak Spanish?
C Yes, but not very well.
P Maybe we can speak Spanish together sometimes?
C OK. I'd like to do that. I think Spanish is *really* difficult.
P It's not for me!
C Ha, ha. No, of course it's not! Do you want to play on the team every week?
P Yes. I love soccer.
C Me too.
P Where's the game next week?
C It's in Albany.
P Is that far away?
C No, it's not far, but you need to drive there.
P Uh oh. I don't have a car.
C Don't worry. You can come with us.
P Thanks! That's really kind.
C No problem. Be ready by 9 o'clock.
P Great. See you next week!

Unit 2

02.01

1 She works as a receptionist in a big hotel.
2 He's a Colombian businessman.
3 My father's an engineer.
4 Jack works as a mechanic for Toyota.
5 My uncle's a taxi driver in Mexico City.
6 Brad Pitt's a well known American actor.
7 My secretary speaks excellent English.
8 She works as a tour guide in Los Angeles.
9 He's a very friendly police officer.
10 Where's the photographer?

02.02

watches
likes
goes
stops
uses
finishes
plays
teaches
works
freezes

02.03

1 **A** Can I have a small coffee, please?
B Of course. Would you like cream or sugar?
2 **A** I'd like some help with my homework, please.
B Sorry, not now. I'm busy.
A That's OK. It doesn't matter.
3 **A** Could you pass me my phone, please?
B Sure, no problem. Here you go.
4 **A** Could we meet tomorrow morning?
B I'm really sorry. I'm not available then.
A Oh, well, that's too bad.

02.04

pound
count
pour
mouse
four
loud

02.05

ALEX Hi, Dan!
DAN Hi! It's great to see you, Alex. How's school this year?
A Not good. It's really hard work! We have important exams at the end of the semester. I have so much homework every day, and my dad still wants me to help him in his store. He doesn't understand how important it is to get good grades.
D You're lucky! My dad *only* wants me to study! He wants me to be a pilot like him.
A And do you want to be a pilot?
D No! I know it's not possible because I'm so bad at math. I always fail my math exams, and you have to pass them to be a pilot.
A What *do* you want to do?
D I want to be a photographer. I want to take photos of famous people and travel all over the world.
A What does your dad think about that?
D He thinks it's a stupid idea. He won't pay for my studies if I do that, only if I study to become a pilot.
A Well, pilots travel all over the world, too.
D That's exactly what my dad says!

Unit 3

03.01

1 I go to the gym twice a week.
2 How often does your brother play football?
3 Caroline eats fruit every day.
4 Do they often go to the Chinese restaurant?
5 We go on vacation three times a year.
6 My brother never does any exercise.

03.02

computer
headphones
tablet
smartwatch
keyboard
laptop
camera
printer
speaker
smartphone

03.03

CHRIS Why don't we play tennis this weekend?
LUCY Tennis? Yeah, that'd be great!
C How about on Sunday afternoon?
L Hmm, maybe. Let me see. Oh, I'm sorry, I can't. I have plans to visit my grandmother on Sunday.
C Are you free on Saturday, then?
L Yes, Saturday's fine.
C Great. Why don't you ask Tanya, too?
L Yes, that's a great idea.

03.04

TOM Why don't we try that new Japanese restaurant this weekend?
LUKE Yes, I'd love to. When are you free?
T How about on Friday?
L Hmm, maybe. Let me see. No, I'm sorry, I can't.
T Oh, that's too bad. Why not?
L I need to work late on Friday.
T OK, no problem. Are you free on Saturday?
L Yes, I am. Saturday's fine.
T Why don't you bring your sister, too?
L Sure. That's a really good idea.
T Great. See you on Saturday.

03.05

1 Why don't we see a movie?
2 Yes, that's fine
3 Do you want to get coffee after class?
4 Can I bring Jack?
5 Here's your coffee, Valeria.
6 Yes, I'd love to.
7 That'd be great.
8 Why don't we try it?

03.06

MATEO Hi, Clara. How are you?
CLARA Hello, Mateo. Fine, thanks. How are you?
M Great, thanks.
C Good. It's my birthday next Saturday. Would you like to join us for dinner at my house?
M Yes, I'd love to. It would be great to see you, Gabriel, and Sergio again.
C Oh, good! And our barbecue is on the 18th. Would you like to come?
M I'd love to, but I'm afraid I can't. I have an important business trip to Quito that weekend, and I can't change it.
C No problem. It's OK.
M I hope you all have a great time at the barbecue. See you on Saturday.
C Yeah, I'm really looking forward to it. Bye!

03.07

SUSIE Look, Adam – I have a new smartwatch. It's great. Now I don't have to bring a lot of gadgets on vacation. Do you have one?
ADAM No, I don't have anything like that. Not even a tablet.

S Really? Why not?
A I don't want to own a lot of gadgets.
S But they're so useful! How do you get the latest news? And what about music? My smartwatch has a really good speaker. I use it all the time.
A Well, I have a laptop, so I read the news on that. But I only have it because I need it for my studies.
S I think you need a smartwatch, too! Why don't we have coffee next week, and I can tell you all the things you can do with it.
A OK, that'd be great. How about Monday, after class?
S Sure. Where should we meet?
A How about the Tin Cup Café? It's on Fourth Street – do you know where that is?
S No, but I can use the map on my smartwatch. That's another reason they're so useful!
A OK, OK. I can see that smartwatches are useful. But I'd love to meet you for coffee, anyway!

Unit 4

04.01

see	parent	meet
hair	say	hate
meat	bear	air
pair	need	play
great	date	sheep

04.02

1 Would you like roasted potatoes or boiled potatoes?
I'd like boiled potatoes, please.
2 Would you like fried fish or grilled fish?
I'd like grilled fish, please.
3 Would you like roasted vegetables or grilled vegetables?
I'd like roasted vegetables, please.
4 Would you like a fried egg or a boiled egg?
I'd like a fried egg, please.
5 Would you like a can of soda or a bottle of soda?
I'd like a bottle of soda, please.
6 Would you like a bag of apples or one apple?
I'd like a bag of apples, please.
7 Would you like a can of tomatoes or fresh tomatoes?
I'd like a can of tomatoes, please.
8 Would you like a bag of chips or a bar of chocolate?
I'd like a bag of chips, please.

04.03

HOST Good evening. Do you have a reservation?
PAUL Yes, we have a reservation for six people.
H Great! What's the name?
P Henderson.
H Yes, I see your name here.
P Can we have a table outside, please?
H Yes, of course. This way, please. Those two over there are both free.
P What do you think? The one on the right?
JENNY I'm not sure. What about the one on the left?
P If you prefer. It's your birthday.
J Well, maybe not. This one's fine.

04.04

A Are you ready to order?
B Yes, I think so.
A What would you like for your appetizer?
B I'd like the tossed salad, please.
A And for your entrée?
B I'll have the grilled steak.
A Would you like steamed vegetables with that?
B Yes, please.
A And for your appetizer, ma'am?
C I'll have the fried fish, please.
A Fried fish with lemon.
C Then I'd like the steak. No, wait. I'll have the lasagna.
B Oh, that's a good idea. Can I change my order?
A Yes, of course.
B I'll have the same. Vegetable lasagna for my entrée.

04.05

1 I'd like the salad and then the steak.
2 Can we have a table for four by the window?
3 Where would you like to sit – inside or outside?
4 Would you like to order now or do you need some more time?
5 I'll have the soup, and the spaghetti for my entrée.
6 I'd like the lamb curry with some rice.

04.06

1 I'd like the tacos, please.
2 Can we have a table by the window?
3 I'd like the mushroom soup for my appetizer.
4 Would you like to order now?
5 I'll have the spaghetti for my entrée.
6 Where would you like to sit – outside?

04.07

KATIE Look at the snow! We can't get out of the house!
TROY Oh no! We can't get to the supermarket. What do we have to eat?
K Oh, Troy, you always think about food!
T But we *need* food. What do we have?
K Let's look in the kitchen.
T There isn't much food here.
K Yes there is. Look, here's some bread.
T And is there jam to go with it?
K No …
T What about eggs?
K No, there aren't any eggs in the fridge.
T Chicken?
K No …
T Yogurt?
K No …
T Well, what can we eat? I'm *hungry*.
K Don't worry, Troy, we have a lot of food. Look … chocolate, onions, bread ….
T But we can't make a meal with them.
K It's OK. I can make something out of them.
T Really?
K Sure. Just wait and see!
…
K Ta-dah! Here's your appetizer.
T What's this?
K Rice and cheese soup.
T Oh, Katie! That's terrible!
K No, it's not! Try some.
T OK, just a little. Mmmm. You're right – it's good. What's the entrée?
K Carrot and fried onion sandwiches.
T I don't believe it! Hmm, I'm not so sure about this dish! Did you make dessert?
K Of course I did – boiled pasta with chocolate sauce!

Unit 5

05.01

1 big	3 pie	5 part
2 put	4 bear	6 pea

05.02

her	door
boring	curtains
furniture	your
airport	certain
dessert	wardrobe

05.03

A Excuse me. Can you tell me how to get to the Grand Hotel, please?
B Yes, of course. Go straight for about 200 meters, then turn left onto Broad Street.
A So, go straight, then turn left onto Broad Street?
B Yes, that's right. Then go straight on Broad Street until you come to Anderson Bank. Then turn right onto Church Avenue.
A So, that's right onto Church Avenue after the bank?
B Yes, then go down Church Avenue for about 100 meters. The hotel is on your left.
A Great. Thanks very much.

05.04

1 Go straight until you come to a subway station on your left.
2 Turn left at the movie theater and go down Cedar Road for 250 meters.
3 Can you tell us how to get to the station, please?
4 Go down High Street for 100 meters, and the concert hall is on your right.
5 Is there a bus stop near here?
6 Go straight for 250 meters, then turn right onto Park Street.
7 It's on the corner next to the bank.
8 How do I get to the train station from here?

05.05

1 Go down Ninth Street.
2 Go straight until you come to the hospital.
3 Can you tell me how to get to the swimming pool, please?
4 Go straight for about 300 meters.
5 Turn right onto Carlisle Avenue.
6 The fitness center is on the left.
7 Is there a bank near here?
8 Go straight for about 150 meters.

05.06

JACK Dan, hi – it's Jack. I'm outside the restaurant, but I can't see you.
DAN That's strange. I'm outside the restaurant, but I can't see *you*.
J What's the name of the restaurant where you are?
D The Panorama.
J Well, that explains it! I'm outside the Flame & Grill. Don't worry – if you're on Main Street, you're very close. Just look for the post office and turn right. Go down that road, and the Flame & Grill restaurant is on your left.
D OK, see you in a minute or two.
D Jack, it's Dan again. I'm at the post office, but you can't turn right here – there isn't a road!
J What? Are you at the wrong post office, too? OK, what else can you see?
D Well, I'm right next to the bridge, so I can see the river. And there's a theater on my right.
J A theater? There's no theater near here.
D But I don't understand. I have your email here, and it says, "Start at Park Place subway station and go straight." I must be somewhere near you.
J Park Place? Does it say Park Place West or Park Place East?
D Oh, no! That explains everything!

Unit 6

06.01

1 My mother was a terrible student.
2 **A:** Was he at work today?
B: No, he wasn't.
3 Were you at the party?
4 We were good friends.
5 Peter was an engineer.
6 **A:** Was he married?
B: Yes, he was.

06.02

1 nineteen sixty-eight	4 two thousand and six
2 twenty fifteen	5 twenty twenty
3 nineteen thirty-nine	6 fourteen ninety-two

06.03

1 closed	6 studied
2 waited	7 visited
3 decided	8 opened
4 arrived	9 started
5 loved	10 worked

06.04

CONVERSATION 1
IAN Hello, this is Ian Smith. I'm not here right now. Please leave me a message.
ABBY Hi, Ian. Can you call me back? You can call me at my work number or on my cell.
CONVERSATION 2
DAVID Hello. Ian Smith's office.
A Oh, hello. Is Ian there?
D Sorry, he's not here right now. He's in a meeting.
A That's OK. It's his sister, Abby. Can he call me back?
D OK, I'll tell him. He'll be back soon. Oh, just a minute. Here he comes now … Ian, it's Abby.
I Hi, Abby. It's me.
A Hello, Ian. Finally!

06.05

1 Please leave me a message.
2 Can you call me back this afternoon?
3 Can you wait a minute?

4 You can call me at work or on my cell.
5 I'm not here right now.
6 Sorry, she's not here right now.

06.06

fall	language	manage
date	draw	email
cottage	happy	ball
am	walk	man
cake	cat	name

06.07

MARIA My aunt and uncle have ten children, and they're all girls.
JAMES Ten girls? That's amazing! How old are they?
M Good question! Well, let's see. Amelia is two. She's the baby of the family. And Abigail is 25 and has two children of her own. In fact, her daughter Brooke is three now!
J So … Brooke has an aunt who's younger than her?
M Yes. It's a little strange, right?
J Not at all. I hear this happens a lot in big families.
M My aunt and uncle always knew they wanted a big family. It's a good thing they have a big house!
J Are you friends with all your cousins?
M Yes, especially the ones that are around the same age as me. When I was a kid, I spent a lot of time with them. We lived near them, so I saw them a lot because they often came over to our house. We played games together, went on picnics, and watched our favorite TV shows. We had a lot of fun.
J It must be a lot of work for your aunt and uncle.
M It is, but my grandparents help out, and my older cousins do a lot of chores around the house.
J So how many brothers and sisters do you have?
M None! My aunt and uncle already had four children when I was born, and my parents looked at them and decided that one child was enough!

06.08

MAGGIE Hi, Tina. How was your weekend?
TINA Oh, hello, Maggie. It was really good, thanks. On Saturday night I went out to a restaurant with Steve.
M Really? Where?
T We went to the new Mexican restaurant downtown. It was really good.
M But isn't it far from your apartment?
T Yes, it is, so we went there by bus. And we went home by taxi.
M Lucky you! Do you want to go for a walk?
T No, I'm sorry, I can't. I need to go shopping. We don't have anything for dinner.
M OK, no problem. Talk to you later.

Unit 7

07.01

thought
south
how
ball
now
law
gone
bought
mouth
house

07.02

1 comfortable
2 dangerous
3 uncomfortable
4 expensive

07.03

1 **A** Excuse me, but I think that's my suitcase.
B Is it? I'm so sorry. I took the wrong one.
A That's OK. They look the same.
2 **A** I'm really sorry I didn't come to your party.
B It doesn't matter. Are you OK?
A I'm all right now, but I didn't feel well yesterday.
3 **A** Excuse me. Can you explain that again, please?
B No problem. German grammar is very hard.

07.04

1 I'm very sorry I'm late. I didn't hear my alarm.
2 I'm sorry I lost your keys. I always lose things.
3 I'm so sorry I broke your phone. I dropped it on the ground.
4 I'm sorry I hit your car. The road was very wet.
5 I'm really sorry I didn't reply to your message. Work was very busy today.

07.05

1 He's very tired today.
2 I'm so sorry I'm late.
3 We're really busy right now.
4 It's very cold outside.
5 I'm really sorry I can't come.
6 We're so lost!

07.06

GLORIA What did you do during summer break, Ignacio?
IGNACIO I went to California. I took my bike with me on the train.
G That's funny – I went to California, too! But I took an airplane from Seattle to Los Angeles.
I I hate traveling on airplanes because I'm so tall. There's never enough space for my legs, so it's always really uncomfortable.
G Oh, I went first class, so it wasn't a problem. Where did you go on your bike?
I I took a train to Napa Valley, and after that I biked everywhere.
G That sounds like hard work!
I Not to me – I love riding my bike through the countryside. You see so much that way. What about you? What's Los Angeles like?
G Oh, it's beautiful, with the beach and hills nearby. And I stayed in a fantastic hotel. It had an amazing pool, and the rooms were beautiful and so comfortable!
I I didn't stay in hotels. I didn't have enough money. I used a website where you can stay in people's homes. It's a cheap way to travel, and you meet lots of interesting people.
G It sounds terrible. I hate staying with people I don't know. And I don't think it's very safe.
I I didn't have any problems. I love meeting people, and I learned so much about California. I often ate dinner with them, too, so I tried a lot of new food. That was really interesting.
G I like to choose what I eat. There are so many fantastic restaurants in Los Angeles. I was there for three weeks, so I went to a lot of them!
I Wasn't that very expensive?
G Oh, probably. I didn't really think about it. I just used my credit card. My parents pay the bill.
I Wow! Do they pay for everything?
G Yes, they do, which is lucky, because I love shopping. And there are lots of great stores in Los Angeles. In fact, I love it so much that on my last day I went shopping and forgot about the time. I missed my plane!
I Oh, no! At least that's one problem I'm sure I'll never have!

Unit 8

08.01

1 **A** What's the matter?
B Nothing. I just have a stomachache.
2 **A** How do you feel?
B Well, actually, I feel terrible.
3 **A** Are you all right?
B Yes, I'm fine now, thanks.
4 **A** Does your knee hurt?
B Yes, it does. It hurts when I walk.
5 **A** Do you have a fever?
B No, I don't. I just feel a little tired.

08.02

TONY Hi, Judy. Good to see you. How are you?
JUDY Hi, Tony. Not so great today.
T Oh, I'm sorry to hear that. What's the matter?
J I'm not sure. I don't feel very well.
T Do you have a fever?
J Yes, maybe, and I have a terrible headache.
T Oh, no! Why don't you go home and go to bed? I can finish your work today.
J OK, thanks.

08.03

1 That man over there doesn't dance very well.
2 I'm sorry, but I can't talk right now.
3 Thank you very much, ma'am. Have a good day.
4 We have a really big garden at our house.
5 There's a small lake in the middle of the park.

08.04

ROSA Hi, Emilia.
EMILIA Hi, Rosa. Are you OK? You don't look well.
R No, my back hurts. I'm sorry, but I can't play badminton with you today.
E That's OK. What happened?
R I was ice skating with my sister, and I fell flat on my back. The pain was terrible! I couldn't walk at all for a few days.
E Oh, I'm so sorry to hear that!
R Can you play badminton with someone else today?
E Yes, no problem. I'll ask Lana. I don't have to be at my next class until two. Would you like to get some coffee?
R Yes, that would be great.
R I'm a little worried about my back. My dad has a bad back, and he has a lot of problems with it. I don't want to be like that.
E Well, my mom has the same problem. She does yoga now, and she says that it really helps.
R Really? That's great, but yoga seems so difficult. And I would feel nervous doing yoga in front of strangers.
E There are a lot of different levels of yoga classes. My mom was in a beginner's class when she first started. She told me that everyone is really friendly, and the yoga teachers are always very helpful. But you don't have to go to a class. There are a lot of good yoga classes online.
R That's a great idea, Emilia. Would you like to try an online yoga class with me?
E Yeah, sure! I need to do something like that. I can't even touch my toes. Can you?
R Well, I could before my skating accident. The doctor says I should be careful, so maybe I should go to a class where a teacher can help me in person, and not online.
E OK. Do you want to go to a class tomorrow evening?
R I can't tomorrow. I have a piano lesson, but what about Thursday evening?

Unit 9

09.01

1 **A** What are you doing here?
B I'm waiting for my brother.
2 **A** Where's Michael going?
B He's looking for his brother.
3 **A** Are you having dinner now?
B Yes, we are. We're having empanadas.
4 **A** What are you buying?
B I'm not buying anything. I'm just looking.
5 **A** It's not raining right now.
B In fact, the sun's shining.

09.02

1 This is one of the biggest shopping malls in the world.
2 There are over two hundred and fifty clothing stores.
3 There are about twenty-three bookstores.
4 If you can't find a store, you can ask someone at the information desk for help.
5 It can be hard to find a space in the parking lot.
6 A lot of people prefer to wait for a bus at the bus stop.

09.03

KARLA Hi, Julian. What are you buying?
JULIAN Hello, Karla. I'm buying some new pants.
K But you usually wear jeans and sneakers.
J Yes, I know. I'm trying to dress well for my new job.
K Well, I like them.
J Good, and, look, I'm wearing some new shoes that I bought yesterday.

K Wow, they look great!
J Thanks. Are you wearing a new dress?
K Yes, I am. What do you think?
J It's really nice. Hey, do you want to get some coffee?
K Sorry, I can't. I'm waiting for my brother. He's parking the car.
J OK, no problem. Bye!

09.04

vote	boat
some	brother
soup	cool
dollar	on
rock	watch
pool	do
other	love
toe	hope

09.05

1 **A** Can I help you?
B Yes, I'm looking for a red dress and some black shoes.
2 **A** Can I try them on?
B Sure. The fitting rooms are over there.
3 **A** What size are you?
B 32, I think.
4 **A** What color would you like?
B Blue or green, please.
5 **A** What do you think?
B It looks really good on you.
6 **A** How much are these jeans?
B They're $49.99.

09.06

1 I'm a size 10.
2 It looks good on you.
3 How much is it?
4 The jeans are over there.

09.07

PART 1

BRAD Uh-oh. Do you see what Dad's wearing?
GLORIA Is that the sweater Grandma made him?
B Yep. The one with the elephant on the front.
G Is he wearing it to be funny on Mom's birthday? Look, she's talking to him now. Maybe she's asking him to take it off before the party.
B No, I think they are just talking about the drinks and snacks. Uh, yep, they are getting more glasses from the kitchen.
G That sweater's so ugly, but Mom doesn't seem to mind. In fact, she seems to be laughing about it.
B Well, Grandma will be happy to see Dad wearing it when she gets here!

PART 2

ANDREW Oh, hi Mom!
GRANDMA Hello, Andrew. I came by early so I could help you and Shelly with the food.
A That's really thoughtful of you. Shelly's in the kitchen making sandwiches. I'm sure she'd love your help.
GR Oh, look! You're wearing the sweater I made. It looks fantastic!
A It's my favorite sweater, and today is a special day!
GR You look so handsome in it!

B Yep, just like we thought – he did it for Grandma!
G Look at how happy she is! Dad really made her day.

PART 3

A Hey everyone, the first visitors are arriving! The party is getting started!
GR Oh! Who is at the door?
A Look! Wanda and Gene are here! Hey, Mom, you know, I'm starting to get a little warm because I'm so excited.
GR The weather today is a little warm for a sweater. You should take it off.
A You're right. Well, I look forward to wearing it tomorrow.
GR OK!

PART 4

B Look, Gloria! Dad took off the sweater, and he's wearing his best shirt under it.
G Very clever, Dad!
B I guess that was his plan the whole time. He made Grandma happy and Mom laugh!

Unit 10

10.01

1 seven thousand five hundred
2 eight hundred and twelve
3 two million five hundred thousand
4 one thousand, two hundred and ninety-nine
5 two thousand and one

10.02

1 English is the most popular language in the world.
2 Suriname is one of the smallest countries in South America.
3 This is one of the most dangerous cities in the world.
4 Brazil is the biggest country in Latin America.
5 Spanish is one of the most useful languages in the world.
6 This is the most expensive hotel in the city.
7 This is one of the saddest movies ever.
8 This is the heaviest thing in my bag.

10.03

A Could you help me with something?
B Yes, of course. What is it?
A I don't know how to record shows on my new TV.
B Sure, that's easy.
A Would you mind showing me?
B No, not at all. So, what you do is this. First you go to the program menu, then you find the show you want, and finally you press "Record."
A OK, that looks easy. Now let me try. So first I go to the program menu?
B Yes, that's right.
A Then I find the show I want with these arrows, like this?
B Correct.
A And then I just press the "Record" button. Is that right?
B Yes, perfect.

10.04

1 **A** Could you help me with my homework?
B Yes, of course.
2 Can you explain that to me?
3 **A** Would you mind helping me?
B No, not at all.
4 **A** Do you mind showing me how to take photos with my phone?
B No problem.
5 So first I click on this link?
6 Next I put in my password, like this?
7 And then I press this button. Is that right?

10.05

1 Can you help me with something?
2 Would you mind showing me how to do it?
3 Could you explain that again, please?
4 Do you mind helping me with my shopping?

10.06

1 How do I check my email?
2 Can you show me how to log in?
3 What's the problem with your computer?
4 Would you mind speaking more slowly, please?
5 Do you mind showing me how to take photos?
6 How often do you check your email?

10.07

Hello! You are listening to *Side Salad*. Today, I want to talk about growing old. There are now more Americans over 100 years old. In 2019, there were about 80,000 people over 100. And in 2014, there were 72,197 Americans 100 years old or older. Just because Americans are living longer now, does it mean they are healthy?
In Loma Linda, California, there is a "Blue Zone." Blue Zones are places that have the highest number of people 100 years old or older. The people who live in Loma Linda don't smoke, eat sugar, dance, or watch TV. They also eat a lot of fruit, nuts, and vegetables. They eat very little meat. The people here are very close to one another. In another Blue Zone located in Costa Rica, people eat mostly beans and corn tortillas. They also work into old age and feel good about life. A third Blue Zone located in Okinawa is the home to the world's oldest women. They also do exercises and eat a lot of vegetables.
So what things do these places share, and why do the people there live to be 100 years old? Scientists think it is because they all do some form of exercise, eat a lot of vegetables, and are close to their friends, families, and neighbors. In other words, they are happier!
But don't worry. If you don't live in a Blue Zone, there are many other things you can do to live your happiest and best life. First, try to sleep 7 to 8 hours every night for a longer life. Right now, 1 in 3 adults are not getting enough sleep, and this causes many illnesses. Second, drink coffee or tea. Both coffee and tea drinkers are in 20 to 30% less danger of early death. Third, keep a healthy social network. This can help you live up to 50% longer. In fact, having 3 close friends in your social network may lower the danger of early death by 200%. So, go out and meet a friend at your favorite coffee shop. And remember, keep smiling!

Unit 11

11.01

1 I've never read any novels by Ernest Hemingway.
2 Have you ever stayed in that hotel?
3 He's driven to Charleston six times this year.
4 Ella and Greg have never met you.
5 Have you ever bought a new car?
6 She hasn't met the president before.

11.02

1 He's a great actor.
2 She's a famous Hollywood movie director.
3 I went to the theater in London last night.
4 She was a well known model when she was young.
5 I'd like to be a fashion photographer.
6 She's won several national prizes.
7 He's the best musician in our family.
8 The orchestra played for three hours.

11.03

TIM So what did you think of the movie?
SAM I really liked the movie. How about you?
T I thought it was pretty good, but it was kind of long.
S Yeah, maybe.
T Did you like the music?
S Yes, I thought it was great.
T You did? I thought it was kind of loud. Sometimes I couldn't hear the actors very well.
S Really? I thought the music was fine. Also, I thought the photography was great.
T Yes, me too. But I didn't like the actor who played Nelson Mandela.
S No, me neither. Anyway, let's go get coffee.

11.04

1 **A** I thought the movie was great.
B You did?
2 **A** I really liked the music.
B Me too.
3 **A** I love going to the theater.
B You do?
4 **A** I didn't like Samuel L. Jackson's last movie.
B Me neither.

11.05

MARIANNE So, Lenny, what's the most interesting place you've been to?
LENNY Well, I've been to lots of great places, but I think Mexico was probably the most interesting. I loved learning about the history, and I've never seen such beautiful beaches before! Also, the food is fantastic.
M What's it like? I've never tried Mexican food.
L Lots of meat, lots of beans, and delicious fruit.
M Hmm. I don't eat meat, so I'm not sure it would be so good for me.

L So how about you? Where's your favorite place?
M Probably Italy. I've been there a few times, and I always enjoy it. I have a friend in the city of Bologna, which has some of the best restaurants in Italy. I think I've eaten in most of them!
L Do you speak Italian?
M Not much. I learned some in school, but I've forgotten most of it now, unfortunately. I'd like to learn again because I really love Italian opera. I've been to the opera in Milan several times, and I've seen some of the best singers in the world. Do you like opera?
L No, I don't really like opera or any type of classical music. I prefer dance music and pop music. I really like a band called Arctic Fire.
M Oh, I've heard some of their albums. My brother likes them, too. And I agree with you – they're great. I like all kinds of music – rock music, jazz – anything! In fact, I think there are really only two types of music – good music and bad music!
L You're probably right.
M Have you *tried* listening to classical music? I think you usually need to hear pieces a few times before you can really understand them. When you know the music, you enjoy it more.
L That's interesting. I'm not sure it's true for pop music. I've bought albums because I liked one song, but when I've listened to them several times, I usually start to like other songs more.
M Well, maybe we can go to a classical concert together one day?
L Sure, if I can take you to see Arctic Fire, too.

Unit 12

12.01

1 In Hawaii, the accommodations are really expensive.
2 I've done a lot of sightseeing today.
3 I like living in the countryside.
4 We have a reservation for 7:30.
5 The nightlife in Mexico City was fantastic.
6 I love traveling to different countries.
7 That restaurant has fantastic food.
8 The scenery in Brazil was amazing.

12.02

1 **A** I won $1,000!
B Really?
2 **A** Thanks for all your help.
B No problem.
3 **A** I'm hungry.
B Me too. When's breakfast?
4 **A** I missed the last train.
B You did?
5 **A** I went to Philadelphia for the weekend.
B You did?
6 **A** Can you call me a taxi, please?
B Of course.
7 **A** There's a parking lot under the hotel.
B How much is it?
8 **A** She's going to live in the U.S.
B She is?
9 **A** I really like opera.
B You do?
10 **A** There's a really good café near my house.
B What time does it open?

12.03

STEPHANIE Hi, Elena.
ELENA Oh, hi Stephanie. I'm so happy to see you. I have some amazing news! Annette is going to buy an island!
S No! How do you buy an island?
E Well, people sell them, just like anything else. I guess it's like buying a house.
S Oh, really? Where is it? And what's she going to do with it?
E It's somewhere in Canada, and I think she's going to build a vacation home there for her family.
S So she's not going to live there all the time?
E Oh, no! There's nothing there. Just a lot of trees.
S That sounds a little boring. She should buy one somewhere warmer. One with nice beaches.
E Well, an island like that is probably a lot more expensive! But I don't think she's interested in that sort of thing anyway. She loves the countryside, and the scenery there is really beautiful. She showed me some photos. When you look across the water from the island, you can see mountains and waterfalls.
S Oh wow! And how do you get to the island?
E Well, at the moment, there's a man who takes them over there in his boat. But they're going to buy their own boat. That way they can come and go when they want to.
S So, how much time are they going to spend there?
E As much as possible, I think, but first they have to build the house! That will take at least a year.
S What are they going to do with the house when they're not there?
E I don't really know, but she said I can stay there if I want to.
S Wow, that's fantastic! You should do that!
E Don't worry – I'm not going to miss an offer like that!

Unit 1

1A

1

a 2 're 3 's 4 're 5 's 6 's

b 2 isn't/'s not 3 aren't 4 'm not 5 aren't/'re not 6 isn't/'s not 7 aren't/'re not 8 isn't/'s not

2

a 2 Brazilian 3 Turkish 4 Mexican 5 Polish 6 Colombian 7 Chinese 8 Saudi

b Across: 7 Spain 10 Japan 11 France
Down: 1 Brazil 2 Russia 3 Germany 5 Australia 6 Italy 8 China 9 Turkey

3

a 2 syllables: Irish, Saudi, Russian
3 syllables: Japanese, Mexican
4 syllables: American, Nigerian, Colombian

1B

1

a 2 Is he 3 Is she 4 Are you 5 Are you 6 are their names 7 Is Enzo 8 Are Joe and Mel

b 2 he isn't / he's not 3 we aren't / we're not 4 it is 5 I'm not / we aren't / we're not 6 she is 7 they are 8 they aren't / they're not

2

a 1 friendly 2 cool, popular 3 fantastic, well known 4 wonderful, kind 5 quiet, great 6 pleasant, amazing

b 2 amazing 3 well known, popular 4 cool, great 5 friendly, wonderful 6 quiet, kind

3

a/b All the words except *chat*, *know*, and *chart* have a /k/ sound.

1C

1

a 2 I'd like to take a fitness class.
3 What's your last name?
4 Can you spell that, please?
5 What time's the next class?
6 It's tomorrow at six thirty. / It's at six thirty tomorrow.
7 Where's the class?
8 It's in Room 3.
9 So that's 6:30 in Room 3?
10 Thanks for your help.
11 You're welcome.

c 1 Hello. How can I help you?
2 Hi. I'd like to take a German class. I'm a beginner.
3 No problem. We have great German classes for beginners.
4 When are the classes?
5 They're on Mondays at 7:30.
6 Great. I'm free on Monday evenings. Can I sign up for the class?
7 Sure. What's your last name?
8 Gonzales.
9 Can you spell that, please?
10 G-O-N-Z-A-L-E-S.
11 Thank you. Enjoy the class.

2

a 2 down 3 up 4 down 5 up 6 down 7 up 8 down 9 up 10 down 11 down

b 2 one 3 four 4 five 5 two 6 two 7 three 8 two 9 three 10 four

1D

1

a 1 d 2 c

b True: 1, 3, 5; False: 2, 4

2

a This is Carlos Ferreira. He's 35 years old and he's Brazilian. He's from Petrópolis, but he studies languages. He takes Spanish classes in Bogotá. This isn't his first time in Colombia. He's very happy to be in Bogotá. He likes languages, movies, and jazz.

Reading and listening extension

1

a 2 d 3 c 4 a

b True: 2, 4, 7, 8; False: 1, 3, 5, 6

2

a 2 a 3 a

b 2 Mexican 3 grandma 4 speaks 5 plays 6 game 7 doesn't have 8 ready

Review and extension

1

2 She really's – She's really 3 Daniela are – Daniela is
4 Im' from – I'm from 5 You are – Are you 6 There – They're
7 **A** Is you – Are you **B** we not – we aren't / we're not
8 **A** Are Maria – Is Maria **B** she's – she is

2

2 amaizing – amazing 3 kool – cool 4 terible – terrible 5 frendly – friendly
6 neice – nice 7 fantastik – fantastic 8 pour – poor

3

2 f 3 d 4 c 5 b 6 a

Unit 2

2A

1

a 2 don't have 3 relaxes 4 doesn't have 5 doesn't watch 6 relax

b 2 doesn't like, doesn't make 3 don't like, think 4 takes, start

2

a Across: 4 police officer 6 taxi driver 7 nurse 8 pilot 9 actor
Down: 2 receptionist 3 chef 4 photographer 5 mechanic

3

a 2 b 3 a 4 a 5 b 6 a 7 b 8 b 9 a 10 b

4

a /ɪz/: uses, finishes, teaches, freezes
/s/ or /z/: likes, goes, stops, plays, works

2B

1

a 1 **B** I do
2 **A** Does Angela study **B** she doesn't
3 do they do
4 do you study
5 **A** Does he have **B** he does
6 **A** Do you listen **B** I don't

b 2 Do you study late at night for your exams? / Do you study for your exams late at night?
3 Do you listen to music while you study?
4 Do they have important exams at the end of this year?
5 How many days a week does she have class?

2

a 2 exams 3 schedule 4 grade 5 notes 6 break 7 study

3

a 2 nine o'clock 3 twenty-five to nine 4 nine thirty 5 a quarter to nine
6 twenty-five after nine 7 a quarter after nine 8 five to nine

2C

1

a 2 e 3 b 4 a 5 d

b 1 **B** Of course
2 **A** I'd like **B** Sorry **A** doesn't matter
3 **A** Could you **B** no problem
4 **A** Could we **B** I'm really **A** too bad

2

a 1 pour, four 2 count, mouse, loud

2D

1

a 3

b True: 3, 5; False: 1, 2, 4

2

a 2 knows 3 break 4 difficult 5 meet 6 week 7 father

Reading and listening extension

1

a 2 doesn't want 3 doesn't work

b 2 in the middle of the day 3 at the end of the day 4 in the afternoon

c True: 3, 5, 7; False: 1, 2, 4, 6, 8

2

a exams, jobs, their dads

b 2 wants 3 wants 4 doesn't want 5 wants 6 wants 7 doesn't want
8 doesn't want

Review and extension

1

2 Julia studies hard on weekends.
3 She speaks Portuguese and Spanish very well.
4 Sam and Ian don't like exams.
5 Does she finish work late?
6 Do Jacob and Sara have a math class at 2:30?
7 My father works as a taxi driver.
8 We know a lot about computers.

2

2 Mrs. Carr works as a receptionist at the hospital.
3 He's an American businessman.
4 My cousin's a police officer in Louisiana.
5 Graciela Iturbide's a famous Mexican photographer.
6 Max works at a five-star hotel as a chef.
7 The taxi drivers in Lima always go very fast.
8 My friend's a mechanic and he fixes my old car for free.

3

2 as, for 3 as, in 4 out of 5 at 6 go to

Unit 3

3A

1

a 2 sometimes watches, often reads
3 always goes, is usually
4 am often, don't usually finish

b 1 They usually have lunch with their grandparents on Sundays. / They usually have lunch on Sundays with their grandparents. / On Sundays, they usually have lunch with their grandparents.
2 I am always tired after my fitness class on Fridays. / I am always tired on Fridays after my fitness class. / On Fridays, I am always tired after my fitness class.
3 My manager often starts work at 7:30 in the morning.
4 His family never has dinner together on the weekends. / On the weekends, his family never has dinner together.
5 What time do you usually go to bed on Sundays? / On Sundays, what time do you usually go to bed?
6 Paul sometimes gets 100% on his math tests. / Sometimes Paul gets 100% on his math tests.

2

a 2 b 3 a 4 a 5 a 6 a

3

a 2 studies, twice a 3 plays, three times a 4 goes, four times a
5 watches, every 6 visits, once a 7 has, three times a 8 works, twice a

4

a 2 stay 3 prefer 4 sells 5 buy 6 find 7 help 8 decide 9 meet 10 cost

3B

1

a 2 **A** Do you go **B** don't 3 does 4 go, goes 5 has, has

b 2 have 3 do 4 doesn't have 5 Does he have 6 does 7 doesn't have
8 goes 9 Do you go 10 don't

2

a Across: 7 camera 8 printer 9 tablet 10 smartphone
Down: 1 laptop 2 speaker 3 keyboard 4 computers 6 smartwatch

3

a 2 b 3 b 4 a 5 b 6 b 7 a 8 b 9 a 10 b

3C

1

a 2 that'd be 3 How about 4 Let me see 5 I can't 6 you free 7 fine
8 don't you 9 great idea

c 4, 1, 9, 2, 7, 6, 10, 11, 5, 8, 3

2

a 2 b 3 a 4 b 5 b 6 a 7 b 8 b

3D

1

a 1 c 2 c

b 2 June 3 with Luisa 4 Monterrey 5 June 22

2

a 2 Hello, Mateo. Fine, thanks. How are you?
3 Great, thanks.
4 Good. It's my birthday next Saturday. Would you like to join us for dinner at my house?
5 Yes, I'd love to. It would be great to see you, Gabriel, and Sergio again.
6 Oh, good! And our barbecue is on the 18th. Would you like to come?
7 I'd love to, but I'm afraid I can't. I have an important business trip to Quito that weekend, and I can't change it.
8 No problem. It's OK.
9 I hope you all have a great time at the barbecue. See you on Saturday.
10 Yeah, I'm really looking forward to it. Bye!

Reading and listening extension

1

a 2 friends 3 questions 4 friendly 5 often 6 end

2

a 2 doesn't want 3 wants 4 wants

b speaker, laptop, smartwatch, tablet

c 2 c 3 b 4 b 5 a 6 a

Review and extension

1

1 My car has new speakers.
2 Look, I have the latest smartphone!
3 She doesn't have a good camera on her phone.

4 Do you have a laptop in your bag?
5 **A** Do they have apps on their phones? **B** Yes, they do.
6 We have a lot of friends in Ecuador.
7 **A** Does Julie have a big family? **B** No, she doesn't.
8 He has a new computer now.

2

2 They go swimming every day.
3 We study English three times a week.
4 My friends and I usually go to the movies about twice a month.
5 My sister goes to the gym once a week.
6 My wife and I go on vacation three times a year.

3

2 in 3 In 4 in 5 on 6 On 7 at 8 at

Unit 4

4A

1

a 2 carrots 3 pasta is 4 some lamb 5 fruit is 6 cheese 7 food 8 milk

b 2 any / some 3 some 4 any 5 any 6 some 7 any 8 some / a 9 a / some 10 any 11 some 12 a 13 any 14 a 15 a

2

a 2 burger 3 lemon 4 grapes 5 chips 6 salad 7 garlic 8 melon 9 cereal 10 pear

b Meat: steak, burger, lamb
Vegetables: carrot, mushroom, onion, garlic
Fruit: grape, melon, pear, lemon

3

a /eɪ/: great, say, date, hate, play
/i/: meat, need, meet, sheep
/eə/: hair, pair, parent, bear, air

4B

1

a 2 She drinks a lot of milk.
3 I'm sorry I don't have much money.
4 My little brother doesn't eat many vegetables.
5 How much fruit do you eat every day?
6 We need a little butter for this recipe.
7 I don't usually drink much coffee in the afternoon.
8 Can you buy a few tomatoes for the salad?

b 2 a lot 3 how many 4 a few 5 many 6 lot of 7 much 8 a lot 9 a little

2

a 2 roasted 3 grilled 4 fried 5 jar 6 bar 7 package 8 bottle

b 2 grilled 3 roasted 4 fried 5 bottle 6 bag 7 can 8 bag

4C

1

a 2 for six 3 the name 4 Can we have 5 This way 6 Those two 7 The one 8 on the left 9 prefer 10 maybe not

c 2 correct
3 What would you like for your appetizer?
4 I'd like the tossed salad, please. / I'll have the tossed salad, please.
5 correct
6 I'll have the grilled steak. / I'd like the grilled steak.
7 Would you like steamed vegetables with that? / Do you want steamed vegetables with that?
8 correct
9 And for your appetizer, ma'am?
10 I'll have the fried fish, please. / I'd like the fried fish, please.
11 correct
12 Then I'd like the steak. No, wait. I'll have the lasagna. / Then I'll have the steak. No, wait. I'll have the lasagna.
13 Oh, that's a good idea. Can I change my order? / Oh, that's a good idea. Can I change my mind?
14 correct
15 I'll have the same. Vegetable lasagna for my entrée.

2

a 2 Can we have a table for four / by the window?
3 Where would you like to sit / – inside or outside?
4 Would you like to order now / or do you need some more time?
5 I'll have the soup / and the spaghetti for my entrée.
6 I'd like the lamb curry / with some rice.

c 2 b 3 a 4 a 5 a 6 b

4D

1

a 3

b True: 2, 4, 5; False: 1, 3

2

a 4, 2, 5, 3, 1

Reading and listening extension

1

a b 1 c 3 d 5 e 2

b True: 2, 4, 6, 7; False: 1, 3, 5, 8

2

a 2 c 3 b 4 a

b Foods Katie and Troy have: chocolate, onions, cheese, rice, carrots, pasta
Foods Katie and Troy don't have: jam, eggs, chips, yogurt

c 7, 3, 5, 1, 2, 6, 4, 8

Review and extension

1

2 I'm sorry, I don't have any Swiss cheese this week.
3 Can I have a bag of rice, please?
4 Yes, we have some eggs in the fridge.
5 Can you buy some bread at the supermarket?
6 No, there aren't any mushrooms in the fridge.
7 We need an onion for the salad.
8 Do we have any milk?

2

2 soup 3 bread 4 lamb 5 vegetables 6 cereal 7 fruit 8 sandwich

3

2 e 3 f 4 c 5 b 6 a

Unit 5

5A

1

a 2 there are 3 There are 4 Are there 5 there are 6 There's 7 Is there 8 there isn't 9 there's 10 there's 11 there aren't 12 Is there

b 1 **B** Yes, there are.
2 **A** Is there a beautiful park downtown?
B Yes, there is.
3 There isn't a subway station near my house.
4 There aren't any stores near my office.
5 There are some cheap hotels near the station.
6 There's a new café near my apartment building.
7 **A** Are there any interesting buildings downtown?
B No, there aren't.

2

a 2 theater 3 stadium 4 police station 5 bridge 6 park

b 2 theater 3 street 4 stadium 5 post office 6 buildings 7 fitness center 8 police station

3

a 2 put 3 pie 4 bear 5 part 6 pea

5B

1

a 2 Our 3 my, theirs 4 Matthew's sister, Her
5 Whose, yours 6 Jim and Anna's

b 1 **B** It's Monica's.
2 I gave my car to my parents. It's theirs now.
3 Her sister, Christina, lives with her. They're identical twins.
4 They have a cat, but it's not theirs. It's their brother's cat. Its name's Brandy.
5 Monica's bedroom is pretty big, but Christina's bedroom is very small.
6 **A** Whose furniture is this?
B Monica says that the couch is hers, but Christina says it's her brother's.
7 Their brother has a new couch. It's really comfortable!

2

a Across: 3 sink 4 lamp 7 couch 10 washing machine 11 stove
12 dresser
Down: 2 wardrobe 5 curtains 6 bookcase 8 armchair 9 mirror

3

a /ɜr/: furniture, dessert, curtains, certain
/ɔr/: boring, airport, door, your, wardrobe

5C

1

a 3, 6, 1, 4, 7, 2, 5

c 2 Turn left at the movie theater and go down Cedar Road for 250 meters. / Go down Cedar Road for 250 meters and turn left at the movie theater.
3 Can you tell us how to get to the station, please? / Can you please tell us how to get to the station?
4 Go down High Street for 100 meters, and the concert hall is on your right.
5 Is there a bus stop near here?
6 Go straight for 250 meters, then turn right onto Park Street.
7 It's on the corner next to the bank.
8 How do I get to the train station from here?

2

a 2 b 3 a 4 b 5 b 6 b 7 a 8 a

5D

1

a sink, stove, couch, curtains, bookcases

b True: 2, 4; False: 1, 3, 5

2

a 2 so 3 and 4 but 5 so 6 so

Reading and listening extension

1

a True: 2; False: 1, 3

b 2 c 3 a 4 e 5 f 6 d 7 b 8 g

2

a 2 find 3 get 4 starts

b post office, bridge, river, theater

c 2 Main Street 3 post office 4 on his left 5 road 6 theater

Review and extension

1

2 My parents' apartment is downtown.
3 This isn't your bike. It's hers.
4 My room number is 127. It's next to yours.
5 Matt and Nick's teacher is Argentinian.
6 Your car is so fast!
7 This isn't our bus. It's theirs.
8 My brother's phone is new.

2

2 The subway station is 100 meters after the bridge.
3 I don't go downtown very often.
4 My favorite restaurant is called Green Hill.
5 There are a lot of beautiful old buildings in my town.
6 There is a nice park near where I live.
7 I never go to the theater on the weekends.
8 The police station is across from City Hall.

3

2 on, across from 3 at the end 4 in front of 5 behind 6 on the corner
7 between 8 on

Unit 6

6A

1

a Evelyn = grandmother, William = grandfather, Joanne = mother, Michael = father, John = uncle, Yvonne = aunt, Sally = sister, Jake = brother, Beatrice = cousin

b 2 grandparents 3 uncle 4 brother 5 aunts 6 sisters

2

a 1 **B** was 2 **A** Were **B** wasn't 3 was, wasn't 4 wasn't, was
5 **A** Were **B** were, was 6 were

b 2 **A** Were **B** were 3 weren't, were 4 **A** were **B** was
5 **A** Were **B** weren't, were 6 was

3

a Yes: 2, 3, 4; No: 5, 6

4

a 2 a 3 a 4 a 5 b 6 b

6B

1

a 1 was 2 was born 3 had 4 liked 5 entered 6 won 7 told 8 joined
9 wrote 10 helped 11 were 12 asked 13 became 14 died 15 received

b 2 stopped, gave 3 was, died 4 found, took 5 went, spent 6 made, ate
7 played, bought 8 worked, got

2

a 2 bought, cost 3 went, had 4 came, brought 5 read, thought 6 got, gave

3

a No extra syllable: 4, 5, 6, 8, 10; Extra syllable: 2, 3, 7, 9

6C

1

a 4 call me back 5 on my cell 6 Ian Smith's office 7 there 8 's not here
9 It's 10 Can he 11 I'll tell 12 back soon 13 a minute 14 It's me

c 2 Can you call me back this afternoon?
3 Can you wait a minute?
4 You can call me at work or on my cell. / You can call me on my cell or at work.
5 I'm not here right now.
6 Sorry, she's not here right now.

2

a /æ/: am, happy, cat, man
/ɔ/: draw, walk, ball
/ɪ/: cottage, language, manage
/eɪ/: date, cake, email, name

6D

1

a 4

b True: 1, 4, 5; False: 2, 3

2

a 2 Four years later 3 in 2011 4 When she was 5 In 2012
6 In 2013 7 In 2014 8 When 9 In 2015 10 a year later

Reading and listening extension

1

a 2 Paragraph 2 3 Paragraph 4 4 Paragraph 3 5 Paragraph 1

b 2 a 3 c 4 c 5 a 6 c

2

a Maria has a lot of cousins. Maria's parents only wanted one child. Maria doesn't have any brothers or sisters.

b 2 child / daughter / girl 3 aunt 4 uncle 5 house 6 spent 7 lived 8 want / have / want to have

Review and extension

1

2 I paid for the meal with my credit card.
3 He ate all his vegetables.
4 They really enjoyed the movie.
5 Were you at work yesterday?
6 The ticket was very expensive. It cost $100!

2

2 He told me his name was Sergio.
3 They made me a delicious chocolate cake.
4 Daisy gave me a ticket for the concert yesterday!
5 Last month, we won a trip to Buenos Aires!
6 I read the paper and then I did the crossword.

3

a 2 to 3 by 4 home 5 for 6 shopping

Unit 7

7A

1

a 2 didn't go 3 didn't take 4 didn't like 5 didn't visit 6 wasn't 7 didn't have 8 didn't check

b 2 did they travel 3 was the drive 4 did the flight cost 5 did she like 6 did you think 7 did he stay 8 did you spend

2

a Across: 5 bicycle 7 scooter 8 ship 9 train
Down: 1 ferry 3 helicopter 4 plane 6 bus

3

a /ɔ/: ball, law, gone, bought
/aʊ/: how, now, mouth, house

7B

1

a 2 traveling 3 driving 4 sitting 5 staying 6 taking

b 2 love, traveling 3 do, like doing 4 don't like taking 5 doesn't mind staying 6 like watching 7 don't mind staying 8 do, love visiting

2

a 2 expensive 3 safe 4 dirty 5 comfortable 6 empty 7 slow 8 cheap

b 2 fast 3 crowded 4 dangerous 5 clean 6 expensive 7 cheap 8 full

3

a 2 <u>dan</u>gerous 3 un<u>com</u>fortable 4 ex<u>pen</u>sive

7C

1

a 2 I'm really sorry. / I'm so sorry.
3 That's OK. / It doesn't matter. / No problem.
4 I'm really sorry. / I'm so sorry.
5 That's OK. / It doesn't matter. / No problem.
6 I'm really sorry. / I'm so sorry. / Excuse me, please.
7 No problem.

c 2 c 3 b 4 a 5 d

2

a 2 so 3 really 4 very 5 really 6 so

7D

1

a 4

b True: 2, 5; False: 1, 3, 4

2

a 2 d 3 f 4 c 5 b 6 a

Reading and listening extension

1

a True: 1, 3; False: 2

b 2 went 3 slept 4 thought 5 find 6 walked 7 heard 8 used

2

a 2 doesn't have 3 doesn't like

b 2 c 3 c 4 c 5 b 6 a 7 a 8 c

Review and extension

1

2 We didn't stay in expensive hotels.
3 I didn't like the food in that restaurant.
4 **A** Did they catch the last bus?
B Yes, they did.
5 He didn't come to the movie theater with us because he was tired.
6 Did you buy your sunglasses in the supermarket?
7 Nick didn't want to wait for the bus.
8 **A** Did he go to his grandparents' house on Sunday?
B No, he didn't.

2

2 We take the train every day at 8 o'clock.
3 Get off at the next stop for the museum.
4 You don't change planes to go to Sydney. It's a direct flight.
5 I didn't get on the bus because it was full.
6 Mary takes the subway to go downtown.

3

2 He gets angry when we're late for class.
3 We got here early today.
4 I got a letter from an old friend last week.
5 I got a new bag this morning.

Unit 8

8A

1

a 2 Can, can't, can 3 can't, can, can't 4 Can, can 5 can, can't

b 2 **A** Could **B** couldn't 3 **A** Can **B** could 4 couldn't, can 5 could 6 can't

2

a 2 football 3 fishing 4 skiing 5 yoga 6 swimming 7 volleyball 8 dance 9 skate 10 sailing

8B

1

a 1 **B** you do, have to 2 don't have to 3 have to 4 **A** Did you have to **B** we did 5 **A** Do you have to **B** you don't, have to

b 1 **B** don't 2 don't have to 3 doesn't have to 4 have to 5 **A** Do, have to **B** do 6 **A** does, have to **B** has to

2

a 1 head 2 neck 3 arm 4 stomach 5 hand 6 leg 7 knee 8 foot

b Across: 6 feet 7 back
Down: 1 toes 2 hand 3 legs 4 foot 5 neck 8 arm

8C

1

a 2 e 3 d 4 a 5 b

c 5, 4, 8, 1, 7, 2, 6, 3

2

a 2 b 3 b 4 a 5 a

8D

1

a 2

b True: 1, 2, 5; False: 3, 4

2

a 2 badly 3 carefully 4 easily 5 well, clearly 6 cheaply

Reading and listening extension

1

a 2

b 2 feet 3 arms 4 ride 5 close 6 tired

2

a True: 2; False: 1, 3

b Rosa: 2, 5, 7, 8, 11; Emilia: 3, 4, 6, 9, 10

c 2 sister 3 hurt a lot 4 dad 5 yoga 6 go to a yoga class

Review and extension

1

2 When I was 15, I could run 100 meters in 12 seconds.
3 I'm sorry I couldn't come to your party.
4 My grandfather can't see very well without his glasses.
5 Can you dance the tango?
6 He couldn't play soccer after he broke his leg.
7 Helen could drive when she was 17.
8 Could you ride a bike when you were five?

2

2 We went running after work yesterday.
3 I love skiing in the winter.
4 We don't play tennis in the rain.
5 Snowboarding is a very popular sport in Chile.
6 I don't like going fishing – it's so boring!
7 I couldn't dance very well before I took lessons.
8 He goes swimming every day before work.

3

2 told 3 say 4 tells 5 said 6 tell

Unit 9

9A

1

a 2 bookstore 3 fast food restaurant 4 clothing store 5 drugstore 6 ATM

2

a 1 **B** 'm waiting
2 **A** 's Michael going **B** He's looking
3 **A** Are you having **B** we are, 're having
4 **A** are you buying **B** 'm not buying, 'm just looking
5 **A** 's not raining **B** 's shining

c 1 **B** 's getting
2 **A** are you waiting **B** 'm waiting
3 **A** Are you and Maria having **B** we're not / we aren't, 're staying
4 **A** are you reading **B** 'm reading
5 's buying
6 are wearing

3

a 2 a 3 a 4 a 5 a 6 a

9B

1

a 2 I'm buying 3 you usually wear 4 I know 5 I'm trying 6 I like 7 I'm wearing 8 they look 9 Are you wearing 10 I am 11 do you think 12 do you want 13 I'm waiting 14 He's parking

c 2 's watching / is watching 3 'm waiting / am waiting 4 drink 5 costs 6 's raining / is raining 7 spend 8 go, 're walking / are walking

2

a Across: 2 jeans 4 socks 7 ring 8 raincoat 11 shorts
Down: 3 skirt 5 shirt 6 gloves 9 watch 10 boots

3

a /ɑ/: dollar, rock, on, watch
/u/: soup, pool, cool, do
/ʌ/: some, other, brother, love
/oʊ/: toe, boat, hope

9C

1

a 2 f 3 b 4 a 5 e 6 c

c 2 I'm a size 10.
3 What color would you like?
4 I think these are your size.
5 The fitting rooms are right over there.
6 They look great on you.
7 I'll take them.
8 Can I pay by credit card?

2

a 2 a 3 b 4 b

9D

1

a 2 c 3 b 4 a

b True: 4; False: 1, 2, 3

2

a 2 Thanks very much for the book you sent me for my birthday.
3 I just wanted to thank you for the flowers.
4 Thank you for the chocolates. They were delicious!
5 I would just like to say thank you for inviting me to your party on Saturday.

Reading and listening extension

1

a 2 city / place 3 neighborhood 4 weather 5 clothes / things

b 2 Italy 3 sister 4 coffee shops 5 fun 6 weather

2

a True: 3, 4; False: 1, 2

b 2 a 3 b 4 c 5 c 6 a 7 c 8 a

Review and extension

1

2 My friend Mario speaks English very well.
3 Sorry, it's time to go because my train's coming. / Sorry, it's time to go because my train is coming.
4 She's waiting for us outside the movie theater.
5 Tony's in that store over there. He's buying a newspaper. / Tony's in that store over there. He is buying a newspaper.
6 I usually go to the movie theater on the weekends.
7 John's at the library. He's studying for his exams.
8 Do you like Italian food?

2

2 The parking lot across the street is open all night.
3 He's waiting for us at the main entrance.
4 The bookstore closes at 5:30.
5 Excuse me. What's the price of these jeans?
6 Here are your T-shirts. The receipt is in the bag.
7 I like your new scarf. It's very nice.
8 My boyfriend bought me these earrings for my birthday.

3

2 took 3 spare 4 save 5 nice 6 spend 7 find

Unit 10

10A

1

a 2 more useful 3 bigger 4 heavier 5 more difficult 6 better 7 easier 8 worse

b 2 bigger 3 better / clearer 4 clearer / better 5 easier 6 more attractive 7 newer 8 more expensive

2

a 2 e 3 d 4 b 5 a

b 2 check 3 visit 4 save 5 link 6 files 7 go

10B

1

a 2 the most popular, to learn
3 the best
4 the noisiest, in the city
5 the strangest
6 the most interesting, in South America
7 the most useful
8 the most famous

b 2 Japanese is one of the hardest languages to learn. / One of the hardest languages to learn is Japanese.
3 Sam is the best student in our class. / The best student in our class is Sam.
4 Last Tuesday was the wettest day of the year. / The wettest day of the year was last Tuesday.
5 She's one of the most beautiful women in the world.
6 Which is the biggest city in the world?
7 Last year we had the coldest winter since 1986. / We had the coldest winter since 1986 last year.
8 The fastest land animal in the world is the cheetah. / The cheetah is the fastest land animal in the world.

2

a 2 c 3 a 4 b 5 a

c 2 three hundred and seventy-nine
3 eight thousand, one hundred and sixty-two
4 four hundred and fifty thousand
5 two thousand and nine
6 seven million, two hundred and ninety-nine thousand, six hundred and twelve

3

a 2 a 3 a 4 b 5 a 6 b 7 a 8 b

10C

1

a 2 of course 3 easy 4 showing 5 not at all 6 looks 7 So first 8 like this 9 right

c 1 **B** of course 2 that to me 3 **A** helping **B** not at all
4 **A** showing **B** No problem 5 So first 6 like this 7 right

2

a 2 a 3 b 4 a

b 2 up 3 down 4 up 5 up 6 down

10D

1

a 2 Helpme2 3 Lizzie39 4 Joe K

b True: 4, 5; False: 1, 2, 3

2

a 2 My new tablet is smaller than my old laptop. Also, it's lighter, so it's easier to carry. /
My new tablet is smaller than my old laptop. It's lighter, so it's also easier to carry.
3 Put in your username and enter your password as well.
4 I can take great photos with my new phone, and I can also post them on social media.
5 He has a new tablet and a new smartphone, too.
6 My uncle gave me a laptop and he bought me a printer as well.

Reading and listening extension

1

a 2 Tip 1 3 Tip 3 4 Tip 2 5 Tip 4

b 2 h 3 e 4 b 5 a 6 d 7 f 8 c

2

a 3

b 2 72,197
3 100
4 20–30%
5 50
6 3

c True: 1, 3; False: 2, 4, 5

Review and extension

1

2 Tablets are usually lighter than laptops.
3 London is the biggest city in the U.K.
4 This hotel is cheaper than the Hotel Classic.
5 It's the most expensive restaurant in the world.
6 Spanish is easier to learn than Navajo.
7 English is the most useful language in the world.
8 I'm not very good at math, but Ian is worse than me.

2

2 I use my smartphone to make calls to my family and friends.
3 I go online to check the weather.
4 You need my password to log in to my computer.
5 Press "Control" and "S" when you want to save your document.
6 It's taking a long time to download the file from this website.

3

2 most of all 3 Most of my friends 4 most people 5 Most of the students 6 most Sundays

Unit 11

11A

1

a 2 has, seen 3 have, read 4 hasn't, acted 5 have, tried 6 have, danced 7 haven't, done 8 Has, been

b 2 Tom Cruise has never won an Oscar.
3 Has she ever written any songs in French?
4 We have never been to Canada before.
5 Have Mel and Tom ever played in an orchestra?
6 I have never met a movie star before.
7 Have you ever had a birthday party in a restaurant?
8 They have never visited the Tower of London.

2

a won, eaten, had, broken, caught, met, done, heard, bought, made, stolen, written, read

Q	H	X	E	N	I	S	F	G	B	D	E	F	G	L
H	Z	F	B	F	H	J	K	E	R	E	A	X	G	K
H	F	M	X	E	J	L	R	Z	O	S	W	R	R	C
E	A	T	E	N	A	N	E	M	K	S	O	G	N	A
A	I	A	H	B	C	D	A	S	E	G	N	N	S	U
R	F	B	F	G	H	A	D	D	N	N	G	S	D	G
D	F	P	R	W	E	F	H	V	F	D	S	U	U	H
B	G	D	Y	O	Y	U	F	B	J	S	S	D	F	T
F	E	H	O	I	A	D	H	J	V	T	V	E	G	G
H	S	E	E	N	P	D	F	B	B	O	U	G	H	T
P	H	H	G	F	E	M	A	G	N	L	K	D	V	R
D	H	L	Y	U	U	A	Q	D	F	E	L	F	D	A
S	Z	A	A	L	O	D	W	D	F	N	R	M	Z	I
F	W	R	I	T	T	E	N	F	G	H	D	D	E	Q
U	T	T	D	F	J	N	G	S	X	U	X	Q	E	T

b 2 seen 3 won 4 broken 5 eaten 6 written 7 read 8 bought

3

a 2 b 3 a 4 a 5 b 6 a

11B

1

a 2 f 3 a 4 b 5 c 6 d

b 2 have 3 've stayed 4 Have you ever seen 5 haven't 6 've been 7 did you see 8 saw 9 did you go 10 went 11 Did you enjoy it 12 did 13 was

2

a 2 a pop singer 3 a jazz musician 4 a classical orchestra 5 tango dancers 6 a rock band

b 2 singer 3 musician 4 orchestras 5 band 6 classical 7 folk 8 pop 9 jazz 10 rock

3

a 2 a 3 b 4 a 5 a 6 b 7 b 8 b

11C

1

a 2 Yeah, maybe.
3 Yes, I thought it was great.
4 Really? I thought the music was fine. Also, I thought the photography was great.
5 No, me neither. Anyway, let's go get coffee.

c 1 **B** I really liked it.
2 **A** Did you enjoy the movie? **B** Yes, I did. I thought the acting was excellent.
3 **A** I didn't like the singer very much. **B** Me, neither.
4 **A** I thought the music was beautiful. **B** Yes, me too.
5 **A** I really enjoyed the concert last night. How about you?
B I didn't like the first half at all, but the second half was amazing.

2

a 2 down 3 up 4 down

11D

1

a 1 b 2 a

b True: 2, 5; False: 1, 3, 4

2

a 2 Daniel Radcliffe was my favorite actor in the movie. He was really good.
3 We want to see the new Studio Ghibli movie. My friend, Andy, told us it is amazing.
4 Alfonso Cuarón is a fantastic director. He won an Oscar for the movie *Roma*.
5 I thought Jay-Z and Beyoncé were fantastic in concert. They are both great musicians.

Reading and listening extension

1

a 2 biology 3 an actor 4 a son 5 is

b 2 live 3 has acted 4 studied 5 earned 6 has been 7 won / has won

2

a places they have been to, food they have eaten, music they enjoy

b 2 a 3 c 4 c 5 a 6 b 7 b 8 c

Review and extension

1

2 I've never seen a movie by Quentin Tarantino. / I have never seen a movie by Quentin Tarantino.
3 They've never been to Barcelona. / They have never been to Barcelona.
4 I've never been to France on vacation. / I have never been to France on vacation.
5 My uncle has written lots of children's books. / My uncle's written lots of children's books.
6 Have you ever read any of the Harry Potter books?
7 **B** No, he hasn't.
8 I've visited my grandmother three times this week. / I have visited my grandmother three times this week.

2

2 I've never forgotten your birthday.
3 No, I've never flown in a helicopter.
4 Have they made a new James Bond film?
5 I've taken lots of photos of the party.
6 No, I've never taken the bus to school. I always walk.

3

2 grew up 3 call back 4 come over 5 fill in 6 try on

Unit 12

12A

1

a Across: 6 rainforest 8 glacier 9 beach 10 lake
Down: 1 islands 2 forest 4 waterfalls 5 mountain 7 desert

2

a 2 f 3 a 4 b 5 c 6 d

b 2 isn't going to take 3 're going to visit 4 are, going to stay 5 Is, going to look 6 Are, going to have 7 'm not going to go 8 're going to come

3

a 1 a 2 b 3 a 4 b 5 a 6 a 7 b 8 a

12B

1

a 2 shouldn't 3 should 4 should 5 shouldn't 6 should 7 shouldn't 8 shouldn't

b 2 She shouldn't walk home alone. It's safer to go by taxi.
3 You should see the new James Bond movie. It's amazing!
4 Where should I change my money?
5 Which countries should I visit in South America?
6 My dad thinks I should go to college next year.
7 They should go to the Gold Museum when they're in Colombia.
8 Should I invite Selena and her sister to the party?

2

a 2 e 3 a 4 f 5 b 6 d

b 2 planned 3 pack 4 booked 5 travels 6 stayed

12C

1

a 4, 6, 11, 1, 8, 7, 16, 2, 10, 13, 9, 15, 3, 5, 12, 14

b 2 h 3 g 4 f 5 b 6 c 7 d 8 a

2

a 2 down 3 down 4 up 5 up 6 down 7 down 8 up 9 up 10 down

12D

1

a 3

b True: 1, 4, 6; False: 2, 3, 5

2

a Opening: 8
Paragraph 1: 3, 7
Paragraph 2: 4, 10, 1, 5
Paragraph 3: 6
Paragraph 4: 2
Closing: 9

Reading and listening extension

1

a 2 c 3 a 4 b

b True: 3, 5, 6; False: 1, 2, 4

2

a 2 beaches 3 countryside 4 mountains, waterfalls

b 2 a 3 a 4 b 5 b 6 a 7 b 8 b

Review and extension

1

2 Are they going to have a party for David's birthday?
3 I'm going to go to college next year. / I am going to go to college next year.
4 I'm going to go shopping with my friends on Saturday.
5 Are you going to spend a week in Costa Rica?
6 She isn't going to study Economics in college. / She's not going to study Economics in college. / She is not going to study Economics in college.
7 We're going to have dinner at a Greek restaurant tonight.
8 Greg's going to go skiing in California in March. He's so lucky! / Greg is going to go skiing in California in March. He's so lucky!

2

2 The countryside in Wisconsin is really beautiful.
3 The biggest waterfall in the U.S. is Niagara Falls.
4 The Sahara is one of the biggest deserts in the world.
5 You can see a lot of beautiful birds in the rainforest.
6 The tallest mountains in South America are the Andes.
7 There were a lot of sheep in the field behind the farm.
8 My dog loves swimming in the lake.

3

2 e 3 a 4 f 5 c 6 b

Acknowledgments

The authors and publishers acknowledge the following sources of copyright material and are grateful for the permissions granted. While every effort has been made, it has not always been possible to identify the sources of all the material used, or to trace all copyright holders. If any omissions are brought to our notice, we will be happy to include the appropriate acknowledgments on reprinting and in the next update to the digital edition, as applicable.

Key:
U = Unit

Photographs
All the photographs are sourced from Getty Images.
Front cover photography by Franz Aberham/Photolibrary/Getty Images Plus/Getty Images.
U1: Marco Rubino/EyeEm; Jose Luis Pelaez Inc/The Image Bank/Getty Images Plus; FG Trade/E+; NicolasMcComber/E+; Thomas Barwick/Stone; Nikada/E+; Hispanolistic/E+; Chaay_Tee/iStock/Getty Images Plus; Orbon Alija/E+; Dean Mitchell/E+; Shapecharge/E+; Westend61; Morsa Images/DigitalVision; JohnnyGreig/E+; Nirian/E+; **U2:** Courtney Hale/E+; Westend61; Gary Conner/Photodisc; Mel Yates/DigitalVision; Ron Levine/DigitalVision; R.M. Nunes/iStock/Getty Images Plus; PhotoAlto/Eric Audras; ER Productions Limited/DigitalVision; Hill Street Studios/DigitalVision; **U3:** Strauss/Curtis/The Image Bank; Yongyuan/E+; Jeffbergen/E+; David Pereiras/EyeEm; Neirfy/iStock/Getty Images Plus; William King/Taxi/Getty Images Plus; Yuri_Arcurs/E+; **U4:** EmirMemedovski/E+; Blend Images - Peathegee Inc; **U5:** Yenwen/E+; Ariel Skelley/DigitalVision; Dmytro Aksonov/E+; Tramino/iStock; OlegAlbinsky/E+; Georgeclerk/E+; Alexander Spatari/Moment; Strickke/E+; Martin-dm/E+; Onurdongel/E+; Ivan/Moment; **U6:** Steve Granitz/WireImage; John CummingThe Image Bank Getty Images Plus; Hybrid Images/Cultura; Ariel Skelley/DigitalVision; Caiaimage; Maskot; **U7:** George Shelley Productions/Photographer's Choice RF; DoraDalton/iStock Editorial/Getty Images Plus; Portra/E+; Vladimir Godnik; Oxygen/Moment; Ajr_images/iStock/Getty Images Plus; Duy Do/Moment; KJELL LINDER/Moment; Anouchka/iStock; Westend61; **U8:** Rachid Chbani/EyeEm; Prapass Pulsub/Moment; Feedough/iStock/Getty Images Plus; RoBeDeRo/E+; Bambu Productions/DigitalVision; Izusek/E+; Umkehrer/iStock/Getty Images Plus; Razvan/iStock Editorial/Getty Images Plus; GlobalStock/E+; Halfpoint/iStock/Getty Images Plus; Mehmet Tay/EyeEm; **U9:** TommL/E+; Mint Images; Kopophoto/iStock Editorial/Getty Images Plus; Csondy/E+; Vera Kevresan/EyeEm; Portra/DigitalVision; Filadendron/E+; Kali9/E+; Mixetto/iStock/Getty Images Plus; Andresr/E+; Tom Werner/DigitalVision; **U10:** Paul Bradbury/OJO Images; Photojournalis/iStock/Getty Images Plus; Martin Harvey; SDI Productions/E+; Plume Creative/DigitalVision; Ales-A/E+; **U11:** Agencyby/iStock/Getty Images Plus; Witthaya Prasongsin/Moment; Trio Images/DigitalVision; Lawrence Manning/Stone; Barros & Barros/Stone/Getty Images Plus; Jianying yin/E+; Viktorcvetkovic/E+; Luoman/E+; SensorSpot/E+; Tara Moore/DigitalVision; Alberto E. Rodriguez/Getty Images Entertainment; Shapecharge/E+; **U12:** Manfred Gottschalk/The Image Bank; Aimin Tang/Photographer's Choice/Getty Images Plus; Sborisov/iStock/Getty Images Plus; Image Source; AntonioGuillem/iStock/Getty Images Plus; LeonU/E+; Jelena Danilovic/iStock/Getty Images Plus.

The following photographs are sourced from other sources/libraries.

U6: Shutterstock/Julie Keen; **U10**: Shutterstock/Voronin76; Shutterstock/Samot.

U1: Commissioned photography by Gareth Boden.

Illustrations
QBS Learning; John Goodwin; Sean/KJA Artists; Alan/KJA Artists; John/KJA Artists; Dusan Lakicevic; Victoria Woodgate.

Typeset by QBS Learning.

Audio Production by John Marshall Media.

Corpus
Development of this publication has made use of the Cambridge English Corpus (CEC). The CEC is a computer database of contemporary spoken and written English, which currently stands at over one billion words. It includes British English, American English and other varieties of English. It also includes the Cambridge Learner Corpus, developed in collaboration with the University of Cambridge ESOL Examinations. Cambridge University Press has built up the CEC to provide evidence about language use that helps us to produce better language teaching materials.

English Profile
This product is informed by English Vocabulary Profile, built as part of English Profile, a collaborative program designed to enhance the learning, teaching and assessment of English worldwide. Its main funding partners are Cambridge University Press and Cambridge Assessment English and its aim is to create a "profile" for English, linked to the Common European Framework of Reference for Languages (CEFR). English Profile outcomes, such as the English Vocabulary Profile, will provide detailed information about the language that learners can be expected to demonstrate at each CEFR level, offering a clear benchmark for learners' proficiency. For more information, please visit www.englishprofile.org.

CALD
The Cambridge Advanced Learner's Dictionary is the world's most widely used dictionary for learners of English. Including all the words and phrases that learners are likely to come across, it also has easy-to-understand definitions and example sentences to show how the word is used in context. The Cambridge Advanced Learner's Dictionary is available online at dictionary.cambridge.org.

CAMBRIDGE
UNIVERSITY PRESS

University Printing House, Cambridge CB2 8BS, United Kingdom

One Liberty Plaza, 20th Floor, New York, NY 10006, USA

477 Williamstown Road, Port Melbourne, VIC 3207, Australia

314–321, 3rd Floor, Plot 3, Splendor Forum, Jasola District Centre, New Delhi – 110025, India

103 Penang Road, #05-06/07, Visioncrest Commercial, Singapore 238467

Cambridge University Press is part of the University of Cambridge.

It furthers the University's mission by disseminating knowledge in the pursuit of education, learning and research at the highest international levels of excellence.

www.cambridge.org
Information on this title: www.cambridge.org/9781108817554

First published 2022

20 19 18 17 16 15 14 13 12 11 10 9 8 7 6 5 4 3 2 1

Printed in Malaysia by Vivar Printing

A catalogue record for this publication is available from the British Library

ISBN 978-1-108-81751-6 Elementary Student's Book with eBook
ISBN 978-1-108-79716-0 Elementary Student's Book A with eBook
ISBN 978-1-108-79717-7 Elementary Student's Book B with eBook
ISBN 978-1-108-85046-9 Elementary Student's Book with Digital Pack
ISBN 978-1-108-86244-8 Elementary Student's Book A with Digital Pack
ISBN 978-1-108-86247-9 Elementary Student's Book B with Digital Pack
ISBN 978-1-108-81755-4 Elementary Workbook with Answers
ISBN 978-1-108-81756-1 Elementary Workbook A with Answers
ISBN 978-1-108-81757-8 Elementary Workbook B with Answers
ISBN 978-1-108-81758-5 Elementary Workbook without Answers
ISBN 978-1-108-81759-2 Elementary Workbook A without Answers
ISBN 978-1-108-81760-8 Elementary Workbook B without Answers
ISBN 978-1-108-81761-5 Elementary Full Contact with eBook
ISBN 978-1-108-81762-2 Elementary Full Contact A with eBook
ISBN 978-1-108-81763-9 Elementary Full Contact B with eBook
ISBN 978-1-108-85051-3 Elementary Full Contact with Digital Pack
ISBN 978-1-108-85054-4 Elementary Full Contact A with Digital Pack
ISBN 978-1-108-86243-1 Elementary Full Contact B with Digital Pack
ISBN 978-1-108-79719-1 Elementary Teacher's Book with Digital Pack
ISBN 978-1-108-79723-8 Elementary Presentation Plus

Additional resources for this publication at www.cambridge.org/americanempower

This page is intentionally left blank.

This page is intentionally left blank.

This page is intentionally left blank.

This page is intentionally left blank.

This page is intentionally left blank.